talking the walk

31 sessions for new small groups

talking the walk

31 sessions for new small groups

Dave Barlett
Bill Muir

Youth Specialties

ZONDERVAN™

GRAND RAPIDS, MICHIGAN 49530

Talking the Walk: 31 sessions for new small groups

Copyright © 2000 by Youth Specialties

Youth Specialties Books, 300 S. Pierce St., El Cajon, CA 92020, are published by Zondervan, 5300 Patterson Ave. S.E., Grand Rapids, MI 49530.

Library of Congress Cataloging-in-Publication Data

Bartlett, Dave, 1949-
    Talking the walk : 31 sessions for new small groups / Dave Bartlett & Bill Muir.
        p. cm.
   ISBN 0-310-23313-5
 1. Church group work with youth. I. Muir, Bill, 1952- II. Title

   BV4447 .B27 2000
   268'.433—dc21

00-035904

Edited by Anita Palmer and Vicki Newby
Cover design by DesignPoint
Interior design by Tom Gulotta

Printed in the United States of America

  02 03 04 05 06 /❖ VG / 10 9 8 7 6

Contents

INTTRODUCTION
7 All about small groups, and how to use this curriculum

MEETING 1
15 Getting to know you

MEETING 2
25 Getting to know all about you

MEETING 3
31 What are words for?

MEETING 4
37 Saying without speaking

MEETING 5
43 Affirm foundation

MEETING 6
47 Facing life's tensions

MEETING 7
53 What's important

MEETING 8
57 I spy

MEETING 9
61 All about me

MEETING 10
65 The beauty of diversity

MEETING 11
71 That's what I like about me

MEETING 12
75 What's important in life

MEETING 13
79 Picture this

MEETING 14
83 Best friends

MEETING 15
87 Family business

MEETING 16
91 Ch-ch-ch-changes

MEETING 17
95 All you need is love

MEETING 18
99 Agree to disagree

MEETING 19
103 The pros and cons of intimacy

MEETING 20
107 Guts and glory

MEETING 21
111 The opposite sex

MEETING 22
117 Let's talk about sex & dating

MEETING 23
121 Pressing concerns

MEETING 24
125 Not perfect, just forgiven

MEETING 25
133 Who's asking?

MEETING 26
137 The substance of things hoped for

MEETING 27
141 Growing up

MEETING 28
145 Encouraging signs

MEETING 29
151 The truth about moods

MEETING 30
155 A friend in need

MEETING 31
159 All good things must come to an end

All about small groups, and how to use this curriculum

[rationale]

The goal of ministry to young people is to help them enter into a relationship with Jesus Christ and live for him. It's a matter of constantly asking *How can I best do this?* One of many ministry methods is small groups—and this book contains ideas and curriculum for just this kind of youth work.

Here's another question adult leaders need ask themselves a lot if they want to communicate with young people: *How can I build and maintain a significant relationship with them?* Faith is caught rather than taught, we're told. When adults look back at their teen years in a youth group, it is common for them to remember not a lesson or talk by that person, but his or her love, attitudes, goals, and faith.

If you want to change the spiritual lives of young people, you'll need to get close and stay close to them. You must honestly and vulnerably share their lives. You must give young people opportunities to sort out their thinking and set priorities with you (regardless of what you think of their thinking and current priorities). You must be willing to accept teens and care about them regardless of their lifestyles and beliefs. You must declare the gospel of Jesus Christ to them in a caring way. These are the goals of small-group ministry.

"We loved you so much," wrote St. Paul to the Christians in the ancient Greek city of Thessalonica, "that we were delighted to share with you not only the gospel of God but our very lives as well, because you had become so dear to us" (1 Thessalonians 1:8). Seldom have the words of a friend meant so much to young people as they do today.

What is different about these small groups?

[definition]

There are all kinds of small groups, with all kinds of purposes—discipleship groups, Bible studies, leadership groups, topical groups, outreach groups. Leaders (or the groups themselves) decide what the groups' goals are, based on the needs of the members.

The material in *Talking the Walk* has been developed as curriculum for small groups with purposes of *reaching out.* Still, much of this book can be easily adapted and used for other kinds of small groups.

What are the unique characteristics of outreach groups?

- Outreach groups consist of 6 to 10 teenagers (preferably coed), who are a mix of non-Christians, new Christians, bored Christians, and committed Christians.

- They meet once each week for 60 to 75 minutes to discuss life issues honestly and realistically.

- Membership of outreach-oriented small groups is determined by the teenagers themselves: they choose with whom they wish to be and from whom they want to learn.

- If they choose an adult leader for their small group—you, for example—then you're an equal participant, who merely moderates the discussion items and activities, and perhaps—if the group as a whole desires it—gives a very brief talk each week. These 5-minute-max talks are the "Says You" sections in the meetings. Just remember that you're *not* The Teacher who always wraps things up neatly. As a leader, you must come to each group meeting also as a learner.

- There is no hidden agenda or preset conclusion for the group to reach. You and the group members are not dealing with a lesson, but rather sharing your lives, hearts, emotions, convictions, experiences, thoughts, and ideas with each other *honestly*. During the first meeting, you must share openly and honestly whatever goals you have for the group.

How do I get people to come to a small group?

[recruitment]

Small-group members are recruited personally by any group members, whether you or students. They are initially recruited for a one-time, one-hour meeting, the idea being that they can give your small group a try and see if they like it. Once the entire group is recruited and has met twice, the individuals are asked to make a commitment to attend three more meetings. Later they might be asked to consider an additional five-week commitment. Members are never asked for an indefinite commitment.

Just remember than an invitation to join is—

- **Enthusiastic.** *This is a new kind of group—it'll be fun!*
- **Personal.** *I'd like you to be a part of my small group.*
- **For a very limited commitment.** *Try it just once.*
- **Interesting and informal.** *We simply talk honestly about life together.*
- **Nonthreatening.** *You are never forced to give an answer—one of our rules is that you can always pass.*
- **Exciting.** *Your friends are there, too!*

When the first meeting time arrives, don't be disappointed if some people don't show up. Even if only three or four people come, go ahead with the meeting. If less than three attend, use the time to explain again your enthusiasm for the group, to demonstrate some of the simple activities, to ask the few who came if they're still interested, and to assure them that *you* are. Agree with the members to recruit someone for the next week.

What are the objectives of this material?

[goals]

In short, to help adult leaders get close to students so they can share with them matters of life and faith. This book will help you build a safe environment where students and leaders can share openly, learn at a fast pace, and be encouraged.

Young people are in the process of discovering who they are and what they stand for. As they listen and share in these meetings, they will continually be addressing their own personal beliefs and values. Your group will become an important and safe arena for self-discovery and the personalization of their values and faith—and probably one of their most enjoyable and valuable hours during the week.

Much of this material is spiritually neutral. It has been written to include non-Christians and Christians alike. With simple changes, it can be used with integrity in both Christian and mainstream settings.

This curriculum is not directly evangelistic in nature, although Christian adults who want to carry the gospel to young people will find many opportunities in these meetings to share their faith. As you continually share deeply from your life—evangelistically or otherwise—young people will be very open to listening about your faith.

If you give a basketball to an adult who cares for kids, everyone will have fun. Give a basketball to an adult who cares for kids *and* is compelled to share God's Good News, and you'll have given that adult a tool for sharing the gospel. This small-group method—and this book—is simply a neutral tool for a leader, like the basketball.

This group curriculum does not have a specific printed goal for each meeting—because the curriculum and specific objectives are not the primary focus. The primary focus is to *identify the concerns and focus of the group*. Sometimes you'll just have to walk away from the agenda in order to discuss what's *really* important to your group members in any given week.

What makes the group work?

[rules]

Three rules help the leader build an environment in which honest sharing and learning can take place:

- **Be honest, or be silent.** The group will never try to force anyone to share. An individual can always choose not to answer by saying, "I pass." Silence becomes a form of honesty that says *I'm not willing to be honest about that yet.* The group communicates on whatever level of intimacy they are comfortable with—but always honestly. The hope is that, with time, your small-group members will share more and more intimately and transparently.

- **Be absolutely confidential.** Practicing strict confidentiality is the only way a group can honestly address anything of importance. Nobody can tell outsiders what is said during a small-group meeting. Betraying this confidence may be grounds for dismissal from the group. Trust is vital.

That having been said, you as the adult leader are required in most states to report some specific kinds of behavior—physical and sexual abuse, among others—even if the behavior was reported or implied in confidence. **You are responsible to know the law.** *And check with your sponsoring organization—be it church, denomination, club, or association—for additional guidelines and requirements you may need to follow. Otherwise you may be held liable by the state or by parents in the case of a crime or a tragedy.*

• **Be committed to attending the meeting.** The commitment of the group members to each other will make this a special time each week.

What happens at the meeting?

[curriculum]

When you lead a small group, you aren't teaching a lesson. Instead, the group—you as facilitator and students, together—discusses personal convictions, attitudes, beliefs, faith, dreams, goals, and lives. The purpose of small-group activities is to help group members honestly discuss life issues.

Much of this curriculum will give your group an opportunity to *practice* relationship skills, rather than just learn about them. Like the ability—

• To be honest with themselves and others.
• To be a good listener.
• To disagree with an answer, while continuing to show respect toward the person who gave the answer.
• To recognize nonverbal communication.
• To give and receive compliments.
• To risk giving vulnerable answers.

This curriculum enables Christians and non-Christians to build an environment in which they can feel safe about speaking honestly. The goal of the curriculum is to bring life issues to the surface each week that you all feel are important. Groups will share significant and honest answers concerning habits, thoughts, goals, faith, and relationships. And the honest environment will dramatically increase the rate of learning.

And, of course, you will need to continually adjust this curriculum to fit your group.

What does the leader do?

[your role]

As a facilitator instead of a teacher, you are an equal participant in the group. Still, group members will look to you the leader as they decide how honest, vulnerable, and open they can be. Your example will model for students how to listen and care. In short, your faith will be caught, not taught.

A small-group leader should be—

- **Enthusiastic.** Verbalize your excitement at the potential of the group and the learning that can take place.

- **Honest.** Share both your personal successes and failures. If you want your students to be real, you must be real first.

- **Vulnerable.** Realize that your failures do not hurt the gospel. In fact, failures—or sin—make the gospel necessary.

- **Learning.** Come to each meeting as a learner rather than as Ms. Answers or Mr. Here's What It Means.

- **Praying.** Pray for your group during recruitment and planning.

- **Confident.** Trust God to work through the group dynamics and the Christians in the group.

- **Flexible.** Tweak the curriculum to the needs of the group—and always look for teachable moments from life.

How do you use this material?

[prep]

Yes, you're just another participant—but as facilitator you're slightly more than that, too. You need to prepare. But take heart—the meetings in *Talking the Walk* have been developed to keep your prep to a minimum. In fact, all you *really* have to do beforehand is understanding the topic of the meeting and something of its flow.

Suggested leader remarks (in boldface) are throughout this curriculum to help you introduce a lesson, reinforce concepts, and encourage discussion. These are suggestions only and should not be used word for word (unless you've had a hard day and don't feel very spontaneous—or prepared, for that matter).

Here's the ideal prep you should do before each meeting:

- Pray for your group members and your time together.

- Read through the meeting curriculum.

- Prepare any needed material.

- Think about your group and make any adjustments that you think would strengthen the material for you and your group.

What will make you a good leader?

[hints]

You'll be a good leader when you care deeply about the individual group members. Young people are keenly able to sense the motivation of their leader. Yet caring deeply is not as easy as it sounds: it takes time and has substantial emotional costs. But caring deeply and communicating that care will make a difference in your group.

It's important to listen closely without making moral judgments about individuals. If you make a judgment on every issue that kids raise, you'll stifle the honesty and spontaneity of your group.

You will find the correct balance between being relaxed and spontaneous on the one hand, and being structured and formal on the other. In fact, the best leaders tend to be relaxed and casual in their approach, yet intense in their beliefs, faith, and values. They seem able to communicate their leadership intensity in an informal and casual way without demanding structure and formal presentation.

You'll want to set the tone for each meeting with enthusiasm and openness. You'll want to lead with honesty, vulnerability, and confidentiality. You'll want to always come to your small group as a colearner, always ready to learn from your group members.

What can happen because of your small groups?

[results]

With God's blessing, a small-group ministry can deeply influence your students —and you. Some results depend on the goals of the leader and the type of the young people involved. Typical results:

- Evangelism, both teen-to-teen and leader-to-teen.
- The ability of Christian teens to verbalize their faith to their non-Christian friends.
- Modeling and discussing biblical values.
- Your better understanding of teenagers and their culture.
- Teenagers' motivation and excitement about their small-group meetings.
- Your modeling of relationship skills to teenagers.
- In your students' eyes, your credibility in ministering to high schoolers.

What questions should I ask myself?

[key questions]

Key questions you, the facilitator, should frequently ask yourself:

- Is my group continuing to learn and grow?
- Are we on a plateau? Are we having difficulty being honest with each other?
- Is this time each week worth my continued involvement as a leader?
- Have I been able to share my personal faith with these young people and challenge them to respond to Christ?
- Are we truly enjoying our time together each week?
- Have our meetings fallen into a rut that we somehow need to climb out of?
- Am I regularly praying for my group members?

- Am I coming to the group as a colearner or have I slipped into the pattern of being a teacher?
- Am I giving advice rather than actively listening?

What is the next step?

[getting started]

Planning, studying, or reading will not teach you how to run a small group. The best way to learn small-group ministry is to simply start a small group. Write down the names of four young people and call them. Share your plan. Recruit them. Ask them for the names of friends or ask them to recruit a friend. Set the time for the first meeting.

Then just *do it!* Jump in! With God's help, go for it. Picture yourself sitting on the floor talking honestly about life issues with five to eight young people. Make a difference in the lives of teenagers. Take the first step and start your small group now. Pray that God will use you in a new and challenging way.

If the curriculum in *Talking the Walk* seems too formidable, don't let it stop you from starting a small group. *You don't have to complete the entire meeting's curriculum each week. What's important is that your group is sharing honestly and openly with each other.* There may be more material here than you can complete each meeting, but don't worry about it. Do what parts fit you and your group. Keep track of what you haven't done, and maybe use it later. Don't tie yourself to the curriculum—use whatever components in each meeting help to open up group members so that they share their lives and their faith.

Are these meeting sequential?

[correct order]

The 31 meetings in *Talking the Walk* are stand-alone meetings that can be used independently and in any order. You as leader choose the topic you think best for a given week. And remember that as you use the curriculum each week, you should nevertheless remain flexible to the needs and weekly events in the lives of group members.

Again, the curriculum is not important in itself, but only as a vehicle to help real-life sharing take place within the group. Don't be afraid to pursue an issue of strong interest to the group members. (Just don't let overlook the curriculum *every* week!)

Will leading a group be easy?

[challenge]

An outreach-oriented group, with a mix of high schoolers with various spiritual backgrounds and maturity levels, can be very effective today. In fact, small-group ministries are consistently one of the best methods for reaching non-Christian and unchurched young people. Teenagers have a strongly felt need to talk and discover who they are and where they are going in life. And as a small-group leader, you can make a major and eternal difference in their lives.

It probably won't be easy. Significant things in life don't come easily. You'll hit some snags, you'll be challenged in your beliefs and values. Yet if you want to help young people, you have to get close to them. And small groups are an effective way of doing just that.

To small-group leaders

[last word]

Small groups can be fun—they have intimacy, excitement, and can attract all kinds of kids. Remember that it's your small group itself, not this material, that will get you close to young people. This curriculum can *help*, of course. But the point of a small group is becoming friends with kids, talking about relevant things, and giving you the opportunity to open the Bible with students. This curriculum is valuable only to the degree that it helps you accomplish these goals.

And pray, of course. And be clear and articulate about your faith and priorities. Challenge kids to respond to Christ. Love them through their inevitable struggles. Be willing to meet with them outside of the small group and allow them to observe how you live out your faith.

The work will be difficult and challenging, but you can do it!

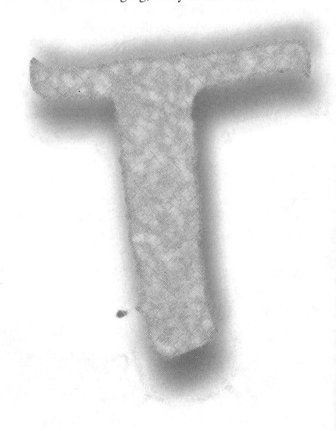

getting to KNOW YOU

The purpose of this meeting is to give you and your group members a chance to get acquainted.

In the beginning *3 min.*

Before the meeting begins, make a copy of the sign on page 20.

You'll need to do two things in the first few minutes of this first meeting. You'll need to make your kids feel welcome and comfortable, and then you'll need to give them an idea of what's in store for them.

Making your group members feel welcome probably will require little more than greeting them warmly at the door and introducing them to others who've already arrived. Having snacks and drinks available helps, too.

Making them feel comfortable, on the other hand, will take some physical maneuvering. The best seating arrangement for a small group is a circle. Ask your kids to arrange their chairs—or themselves, if you've got a group of floor sitters—in a circle. That way, all of your group members will have face-to-face contact with each other.

To give your kids an idea of what's in store for them in this small group setting, you may want to go over a few guidelines for maximum group effectiveness. You can show the sign as you're talking or pull it out when you're finished and post it where everyone can see it and you can refer to it whenever necessary. You might explain the guidelines this way—

This small group is a place where we can get to know each other and, at the same time, learn some important things about ourselves. To make the most of our time together, we'll need to keep three things in mind:

> **For this meeting you'll need...**
>
> • A copy of the sign on page 20
> • A Bible
> • A copy of **Question Time** (pages 21-23), cut into strips

trade secret
Food and drinks are a great way to distract people from the discomfort they may initially feel when arriving. You won't have to worry about competing with the sound of growling stomachs throughout the meeting either. You're guaranteed to be a hero in your group members' eyes—at least for as long they're eating. You may want to provide food every week.

trade secret
Finding a comfortable closeness is vital to your group's interaction. You want your group members close enough together to feel like they're part of a group, but far enough apart to prevent any personal space violations. A good indicator of comfortable closeness is legroom. If your kids have enough room to cross and uncross their legs without kicking the people next to them, they're comfortably close.

trade secret
Your kids take their cues from you—at least in the beginning of your time together. That's why it's important for you to be enthusiastic. If your group members can spot your excitement about the possibilities that lie ahead for your group, they're more likely to get excited themselves.

First, *be honest or be quiet.* In this group, you'll never have to answer a question that you don't want to answer. If you don't feel like responding to something, just say, "I pass." If you *do* feel like responding, though, make sure your answers are completely honest. It may be difficult at first, but with a little practice we'll all get the hang of it.

Second, *what's said here stays here.* Total confidentiality is a must. Everything we share during our time together is private. None of us is allowed to talk about it outside of this group. That way we can all feel comfortable about talking honestly and openly together.

Third, *commitments must be kept.* If we decide that this small group is something we're interested in, we must make it a priority in our lives.

share and share alike   15 min.

Ask your group members to choose three things they're either wearing or carrying that reveal something about them. Potential items might include a driver's license, a necklace, athletic shoes, or a school I.D. If you've got kids who travel lightly and don't have three such items on them, let them point out physical characteristics that reveal something about them. (For example, some kids may point to their red hair to explain their fiery tempers. Others may display telltale scars.)

As the leader of the group, it's your responsibility to blaze a trail for your group members. That's why you'll need to be prepared to share three items that reveal something about you. You may want to use this opportunity to model openness and vulnerability to your kids. Find an item that reveals something embarrassing or unflattering about yourself. You'll discover that the ability to laugh at yourself will go a long way toward connecting with your group members.

After you've finished sharing, ask for a volunteer to go next. When that person is finished, continue until everyone has had a turn.

Buddy up   10 min.

After the group sharing activity, give your kids a chance to become better acquainted on a personal level. Assign everyone in the room—including yourself—a partner. Your best bet is to pair up people who don't know each other well. Encourage each pair to separate itself from the rest of the group as much as possible. Explain the activity this way—

In your pairs, one of you will be the designated questioner and one will be the designated answerer. It doesn't matter which of you chooses which role, because you'll be switching in a few minutes anyway. Those of you who have experience as journalists should do well as questioners. Those of you who have experience as celebrities should do well as answerers.

trade secret

All the sharing in the world won't mean a thing if your kids don't *listen* to each other. Throughout this activity, emphasize the importance of listening and finding out new things about each other. Model good listening skills by asking appropriate questions after each person shares. Focus intently on each speaker, maintaining consistent eye contact and responding as situations dictate.

trade secret

As one of the participants in the activity, you have a golden opportunity to get to know one of your group members in a brief one-on-one situation. Make the most of it. Prepare a mix of questions ahead of time that are revealing, but nonthreatening—questions that will give you a better understanding of your partner without sounding like an interrogator.

trade secret

Youth Specialties has published several books of conversation-starting questions that you can use for creative questions: *Unfinished Sentences, What If...?, Would You Rather...?,* and *Have You Ever...?* They're useful resources for questions throughout these sessions.

Think of this activity as an interview. The questioners will have three minutes to find out as much as possible about the answerer. As far as the questions are concerned, you're on your own. Ask whatever you'd like to know about your partner. Of course, if you get too personal, your partner can always say, "No comment."

Here are a few ideas to get you started.

- **If you were principal of your school for a day, what would you change and why?**
- **When you get older, do you think you'll stay in this area or head for some place far, far away?**
- **If you had a pocketful of money and absolutely no responsibilities, where would you go and what would you do?**

After three minutes, reassemble the group. Ask your designated questioners to share two or three important things they learned about their partners. If you were the designated partner in your group, take the lead in sharing to give your group an idea of what you're looking for.

After everyone has had a chance to share, split up into the same pairs again and have the partners switch roles. Those who were asking the questions before will now be answering them. After three minutes, bring the group back together and give the new questioners a chance to share what they learned about their partners.

Finish the— *10 min.*

Use the following statement—or something like it—to make the transition to your next get-acquainted activity.

We've got such interesting people in this group! Let's find out some more stuff about each other. I'm going to read the beginning of a sentence, and I want you to finish it. These aren't right or wrong statements, so you don't have to worry about making a mistake. We're just looking for your honest response.

Read each of the following statements one at a time. After you read the first statement, finish it with your own personal answer. Then ask your kids to do the same thing. After everyone has completed the first one, move on to the second. Continue until you and all of your kids have responded to all five statements.

1. **The reason I'm here right now is—**
2. **One fear I had in coming here is—**
3. **One thing I'm really excited about in my life right now is—**
4. **One thing about me you probably don't know is—**
5. **One area of my life in which I'm proud of myself is—**

trade secret
You'll be setting the pace for your group members in this activity. The more openness, honesty, and vulnerability you show in responding to these statements, the more likely your kids will be to share their true feelings. Remind your group members that they have the option to pass if they're not comfortable with responding to a statement.

trade secret
Your meeting should last no longer than an hour. If you need to save time somewhere in the session, this is the place to do it. Rather than having your kids continue drawing slips until all have been answered, simply go around the circle one time.

So many questions, so little time *10 min*

You'll find **Question Time** on pages 21-23. Before the meeting starts, make a copy of the sheet and cut apart the questions. For this activity, place the question slips upside down in a pile in the middle of the group. To start things off, you should draw a slip and answer the question. After you've finished answering, ask the person on your right to draw a question and answer it. Continue around the circle until everyone has had a chance to draw one or more questions.

Remind your group members that they may decline to answer any question they're uncomfortable with. If people choose not to answer the first question they drew, they should be allowed to draw a second slip. If they choose not to answer that question either, they may forfeit their turn.

You'll use these questions again, so don't throw them away.

Says you *5 min*

The role of a small group leader carries with it a fair share of opportunities and responsibilities. For example, you'll have the opportunity to flesh out the Christian life for your kids. At the same time, however, you'll have the responsibility of presenting an accurate, warts-and-all view of what it means to follow Christ.

As the small group leader, you'll also have the opportunity to share at least one significant idea with your kids each week. For this first meeting, you might consider sharing some of the following thoughts.

trade secret
Use these suggestions as a general outline, not as a script. Wherever possible, substitute your own words or add relevant examples from your own life or references that will mean something to your group members.

I'm really glad you took time from your busy schedules to check out our small group. I hope that we can continue to meet and get to know each other better and better. I think I can learn a lot from you, and I hope you can learn at least a little from me. I'd love for us to be able to talk honestly and openly about many different topics.

One of the most important things you should know about me is that I'm a committed Christian. At some point in our friendship, I'd like to discuss your thoughts about the Christian faith. I'll be honest about what I believe, and I hope you'll do the same. While we're talking about the Christian faith, let me read you a couple of Bible verses I've been thinking about lately.

If some of your group members are packing Bibles, ask one of them to read 2 Corinthians 5:17-19. If not, read it yourself. Then continue with something like this—

Therefore, if anyone is in Christ, he is a new creation; the old has gone, the new has come! All this is from God, who reconciled us to himself through Christ and gave us the ministry of reconciliation: that God was reconciling the world to himself in Christ, not counting men's sins against them. And he has committed to us the message of reconciliation.

—2 Corinthians 5:17-19

This passage is a summary of how I see my life. I think of myself as an agent of Christ. One of the most important parts of my life is sharing the message of Christ. I don't want to push it on anyone or shove it down someone's throat, but I do want people to know it's important to me.

As you get to know me, you may notice that a lot of my thinking is influenced by my faith. I believe that Jesus is a real, living person; therefore, I'm going to do everything I can to be an ambassador for him.

Did you hear that? *10 min*

So far, you've led your group members through several sharing exercises. As you wrap up the session, try a listening activity. After all, you want your kids to believe that the thoughts, feelings, and experiences they share in your meetings are important to the rest of the group.

To do this, lead your kids in a listening check. Choose one person from the group to focus on at a time. You and your group members should then take turns recalling information you learned about the person or memorable things that person said during the meeting. Ideally, everyone in the group should contribute at least one recollection to the activity. If that doesn't happen, though, don't worry about it. (After all, this *is* your first meeting. In time your group members will get the hang of active listening.)

Again, you'll probably need to take the lead in this exercise. Choose one person from the group and say something like this—

Carlos, the one comment of yours that stands out in my memory is your great description of what a true friend is.

Make sure you comment on a specific idea that the person shared. After you start the ball rolling, encourage your group members to follow suit, commenting on the verbal contributions they remember the person making to the meeting. After all or most of your kids have shared, choose another person in the group to focus on. Continue until everyone has had a turn in the spotlight.

Where do we go from here? *2 min*

Now that you've reached the end of your first meeting, it's time to find out if your kids are interested in meeting again. After all, this first meeting was probably an experiment for some of them, especially if you recruited them to attend. You might approach the situation this way—

I've enjoyed this session, and I'd be interested in meeting again with anyone who wants to. I should warn you, though, that if you want to be a part of this group, it's going to require a commitment on your part. Our meeting times are going to have to become a priority in your life. We can make a difference in each other's lives—and in the community around us—but only if we're serious about meeting together regularly. If you're not interested in that kind of a commitment, just say so. It's okay, and no one will hassle you about it.

If your kids decide to continue meeting together, set up the time and place of your next meeting.

trade secret
If time gets tight at the end of your meeting, you may be tempted to skip this section. *Don't.* This activity is important because it helps kids recognize that the others in the group are actually paying attention to them.

trade secret
For that extra personal touch, you might consider calling, writing a note, or sending an e-mail message to each of the group members who attended your first meeting. You don't need to do anything formal. Just let all the kids know that you're glad they came to the meeting, that you're thinking about them, and that you're always available to talk.

Be honest or be quiet.

~

What's said here stays here.

~

Commitments must be kept.

?????Question time?????

Cut the questions into strips. Use the questions as directed in Meetings 1, 2, and 5 activities.

Who is your favorite teacher and why?

Name something that easily embarrasses you.

Give someone an honest piece of advice.

When do you pray the hardest?

Say something about a topic you're uncomfortable with.

Name one area in which you need to grow up.

Name something you've learned about yourself recently.

What's the most important thing about being a Christian?

Name and describe one of your personal heroes.

What hurts you?

Who in this group would you be willing to depend on and why?

Name one area in which you want to be like your parents.

Name one activity or area in which you would like to be better than everyone else.

Say something about your partying habits.

Say something about Florida *(or choose another state)*.

Say something about traveling.

Say something about this small group.

21

Describe a good friend.

Tell us about your favorite movie of all time.

What makes you laugh out loud?

How do you feel about writing letters?

In what way do you wish people your age would change?

Why are friends important to you?

What do you like most about your parents?

What are most of your arguments with your parents about?

Name one thing you wish your parents would let you do.

Finish this sentence: Home should be a place that—

What kind of people do you like most?

What kind of people are most difficult for you to get along with?

In what ways are your friends like you?

How do you think your parents would describe you?

If you had one wish, what would it be?

What would you like the courage to do?

What is one thing that frightens you?

What do you feel uncomfortable talking about?

What one thing do you think you need the most?

What do you think about when you're all alone?

What's the thing you worry about most?

What do you do when you're sad?

When you're happy, how can people tell?

What is your weakest point?

What do you love to do?

What are you feeling right now?

When are you the happiest?

If you could ask God one question, what would it be?

What's the one thing you like best about yourself?

Finish the sentence: To me, Jesus Christ is—

What do you want to be doing in 10 years?

How would you describe success?

How do you feel when someone calls you names?

Describe the ideal mother.

Who has helped you the most in your life?

Say something about ghosts.

Are you more of a leader or a follower? Why?

What are some of the rules of your house?

What is your definition of sin?

When do you feel the most alone?

Talk about one of your bad habits.

How well do your parents understand you?

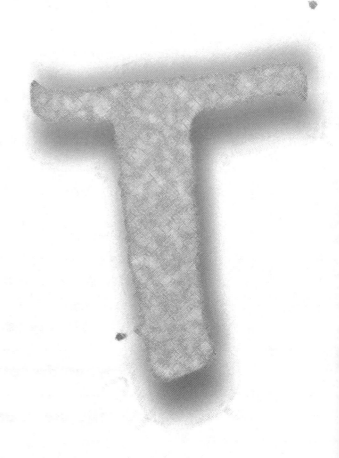

getting to know ALL about YOU

The purpose of this meeting is to build trust among your group members so they're willing to be open and honest with each other.

In the beginning *3 min*

Start off the meeting by arranging your seating in a conversation-friendly circle. Encourage everyone to join the circle. If at all possible, make sure no one physically separates himself from the group by sitting away from the circle.

For the sake of newcomers and group veterans alike, you'll want to go over the three tips for group interaction you introduced at your last meeting (motion toward the sign you posted during the last session)—

This group is a place where we can get to know each other and get to know ourselves. To get the most out of our time together, we need to remember three things:

Be honest or be quiet. **In this group, you'll never be forced to answer a question. If you don't feel like answering, just say, "I pass." If you *do* feel like answering, though, do it honestly. It may be tough at first, but with a little practice we'll get the hang of it.**

What's said here stays here. **Everything we talk about during our time together is private. No one is allowed to talk about it apart from this group. Remember, we all want to feel comfortable about sharing honestly and openly.**

Commitments must be kept. **If this small group is something we're interested in, we have to make it a priority. In other words, we have to show up each week.**

trade secret
If you have new people at your meeting, make them feel comfortable. Before the meeting, introduce yourself and any group members who happen to be nearby. Find out what you can about your newcomers and use that information when you officially introduce them to the group at the beginning of your meeting. Encourage the rest of your group members to include the newcomers in their conversations and activities.

For this meeting you'll need...

- Index cards
- Pencils
- A copy of **Question Time** from the last lesson (pages 21-23), cut into strips

trade secret
It's one thing to give permission to say, "I pass," in response to an uncomfortable question; it's another thing to create an atmosphere in which kids are comfortable doing so. Make sure that you give your group members positive reinforcement when they have the courage to say, "I pass."

Picture this 20 min

Hand out index cards and pencils. Give your kids instructions like these—

> I want you to divide your card into six sections—not by tearing it apart, but by drawing lines. When you're finished with that, number the sections one through six. Here's the way this activity works. I'll ask you six questions. Rather than *writing* a response to each question, though, I want you to draw a symbol that represents your answer.
>
> Don't tell anyone what your symbols mean, and don't worry if you're not the world's greatest artist. We're not going to hang your drawings in a gallery. The purpose of the symbols is simply to remind *you* of your answers.

Ask the following questions one at a time, giving group members time to draw their responses to each one.

> 1. Which person in your life can you be most honest with?
> 2. What's one of your biggest fears?
> 3. What's one talent or skill that you possess?
> 4. What are your friends like?
> 5. What's your bedroom like?
> 6. What do you think about church?

trade secret
Group leaders don't get to be spectators during this activity. Grab an index card and pencil and draw with your kids. Make sure you give honest, thoughtful answers. The more open and vulnerable you are in your responses, the more open your kids will be in their answers.

If your group members struggle with a response to one or more of the questions, assure them that it's not a problem. No one will mind if they can't think of a symbol for each question. After everyone is finished, explain the sharing part of the activity this way—

> We're going to share the symbols we wrote down, but we're going to do it in four different rounds. I'll start each round, and then we'll go around the circle to the right. Each round I'll ask you to share a different symbol. You can tell us as much or as little as you want about each symbol. Whatever you do, though, make sure that you don't get so caught up in sharing your own symbols that you forget to listen to what everyone else is saying.
>
> Round One. Share with the group the symbol that popped into your head the quickest.

trade secret
When you share your symbol, make sure you don't monopolize the conversation. After all, chances are you're already doing lots of the talking in the meeting. Give others a chance!

Show your index card to the group, pointing out the appropriate symbol. Explain what it is, what it represents, and why you think it popped into your head so quickly.

After you've shared, invite the person on your right to do the same, and continue around the circle. Repeat the same process for the other three rounds, using these suggestions for how to introduce them.

Round Two. Share with the group the symbol that you think would surprise us most.

Round Three. Share with the group the symbol that calls for the most openness and honesty on your part.

Round Four. Share with the group the symbol of your choice.

After you've gone through four rounds of sharing, make a transition to the next part of your meeting. You might say something like this—

Those were some pretty interesting symbols. You guys are better artists than I expected! You're also pretty good at opening up and being honest with each other. Let's see if we can maintain that same openness in our next activity.

So many questions, so little time *20 min*

For this activity you'll need the **Question Time** slips (pages 21-23) you used during the last meeting. Shuffle the question slips and deal them to your group members—and yourself—one at a time until all of them are gone. Depending on the size of your group, everyone should have four to seven slips. Explain the activity this way—

The first thing I want you to do is look through the questions you've been dealt and choose one of them to answer in front of the group.

Give your kids a minute or so to choose a question, then at random ask them to respond when they're ready. After everyone has answered a question, move on to the second part of the activity. Tell the kids to look at their slips again, and decide which question they'd like the person on their left to answer

Give your kids a minute or so to choose a question. This time start the round by choosing a question for the person on your left. Remind your group members everyone is free to say, "I pass."

After the person on your left answers the question you chose, the student chooses a question for the next student to the left. Continue this pattern around the circle until everyone has had a chance to respond.

If you've got some extra time at the end of the activity and your kids seem to be enjoying themselves, you might try another round, in which kids choose questions for the person on their right. Another possibility would be to have kids choose questions for the group member of their choice. (Save the question slips for a future meeting.)

Says you *5 min*

The fact that you care enough about your group members to listen to them and encourage them earns you the right to share your thoughts and feelings with

trade secret
Keep your ears open during this activity and you may discover some things about your group members that will help you connect with them later. Even seemingly insignificant details may turn out to be important. If you don't trust your memory, jot down some notes.

them. Take advantage of this hard-earned right by using five minutes of your meeting time to talk about some things that are close to your heart—things that will make a difference in your kids' lives.

Below you'll find a sample narrative to give you an idea of some things you might share with your group members. The purpose of the sample is merely to get you thinking. The things you share with *your* group members should come straight from *your* heart. Think about what it is that you want your kids to take away from the meeting. Whatever you choose to discuss, make sure that your talk clocks in at under five minutes. Any longer than that, and you'll be trying your kids' patience and attention span.

I'm really enjoying our time together, and I hope you are, too.

Sometimes, though, I wonder what you guys think of me when I give a totally honest answer about myself. Sometimes honesty makes you vulnerable, and it's hard to make yourself vulnerable in front of other people—even in a small group setting. The good news, though, is that we're learning a lot about each other and ourselves. So I want to thank you not only for making this meeting a priority, but also for your willingness to be honest.

I'd like to share a Bible verse with you. It was written by the apostle Paul to some Christian friends he'd spent time with. The verse is 1 Thessalonians 2:8, and it goes like this: "We loved you so much that we were delighted to share with you not only the gospel of God but our lives as well, because you had become so dear to us."

Why did I choose this verse? Because I think it describes what we're doing together. We're honestly sharing our lives. I'll admit that I'm interested in sharing my Christian beliefs, but I'm also interested in sharing my life. That includes my feelings, thoughts, and struggles.

I think we'll learn both by listening and by sharing. You might want to think of our small group time as practice for being real people. We have a lot of learning ahead of us—about each other, about God's Word, and about ourselves. If we're honest and caring with each other, I believe God will be pleased.

Did you hear that? *10 min*

Before you wrap up this session, lead your kids in the same listening activity you used in your last meeting. Choose one person from the group to focus on at a time.

To start the exercise, choose one person from the group and say something like this—

Kelly, today I learned that one of your biggest fears is speaking in front of a crowd. I also learned that you're brave enough to overcome that fear because you chose to share with the group.

You and your kids should then take turns listing some other contributions the person made during the meeting. If possible, see to it that everyone in the group contributes at least one recollection. If that doesn't happen, though, don't sweat it. After most of your kids have shared, choose another person in the group to focus on. Continue until everyone has had a turn in the spotlight.

Where do we go from here? *2 min*

The kids in your group who chose to return for this second meeting demonstrated the first signs of commitment. As you wrap up this session, take a few minutes to discuss the level of commitment necessary for a successful small group. Ask your kids if they would be willing to commit to three more meetings in order to really get to know each other on a deep level.

If your kids commit to three more weeks, set up the time and place of your next meeting.

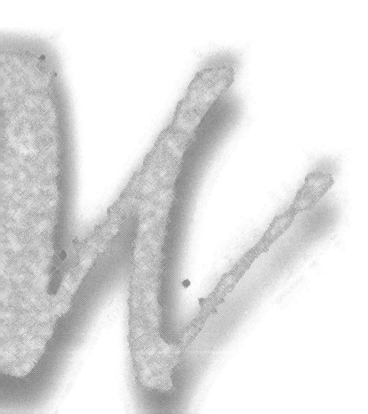

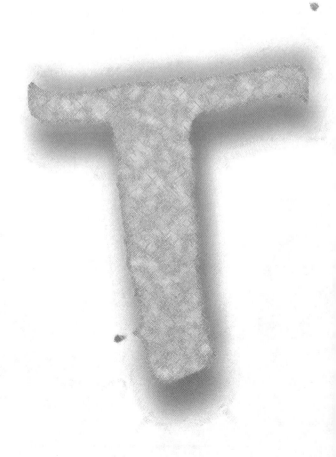

what are WORDS for?

The purpose of this meeting is to sharpen your group members' skills in communicating and listening.

In the beginning *3 min*

Before the meeting, recruit a volunteer from the group to help you with a brief demonstration. The only equipment you'll need for the demonstration is a tennis ball. Secretly explain to your helper that you will throw the ball to him or her, and that the helper should *not* throw it back to you, regardless of how much you request it.

At the beginning of the meeting, throw the ball to your recruit. After the person catches it, motion for him or her to throw it back to you. When the volunteer doesn't, walk over and take the ball back. Then throw it to again. Go through the same routine again. Continue this pattern a few times until the rest of your group members get a little restless.

Discuss the demonstration by asking a question like this—

How long do you think you'd enjoy a game of catch like the one you just saw? Why?

You'll want to get across the point that unless you're trying to teach someone how to catch and throw, a one-sided game of catch would be pretty dull and pointless. Then continue.

What are some other things that require two people?

> ### For this meeting you'll need...
>
> - A tennis ball
> - A bag filled with the following items (or reasonable substitutes): a family photo, a house from a Monopoly game, a school book, a paycheck stub, a road map, a fishing pole, a light bulb, and a college application
> - A Bible

trade secret
Review the three tips for group interaction as often as necessary.

If no one mentions it, suggest that a conversation must have at least two people to be a conversation. Then ask something like—

Have you ever tried to carry on a conversation with someone who wasn't interested in talking or didn't have much to say? Have you ever tried to talk with someone who only gave one-word answers? What's it like?

Encourage several kids to share their experiences. Be sure someone makes the comparison with the game of catch you just demonstrated, with one person doing all of the work.

Conversation Pieces *(20 minutes)*

Take a quick poll of your group members. Ask them to respond to this question—

What's the most important thing to remember when it comes to starting a conversation with someone?

Your kids will likely mention such things as maintaining good eye contact and calling the person by name as much as possible.

If no one else mentions it, suggest that perhaps *the* most important thing to remember when it comes to starting a conversation is this: *Have something to talk about!* It may seem like an obvious statement, but you may be surprised by the number of people who are clueless about what to say to another person.

The following activity is designed to help introduce your group members to some useful conversation topics. You'll need a bag filled with these items (or reasonable substitutes): a family photo, a house from a Monopoly game, a school book, a paycheck stub, a road map, a fishing pole, a light bulb, and a college application.

Explain the activity with a statement like this—

I'm going to pass this bag around the circle. I want you to pull out an item and try to guess the conversation topic that the item represents.

Dig through the bag for the family photo. Pull it out and display it to the group, and continue—

For example, this picture represents family. A great way to start a conversation with people is to ask about their families. Does she have any brothers or sisters? If so, is she the oldest, the youngest, or a middle child? How does she feel about it? Is she more like her mom or her dad? The more you get to know about her family, the more things you may find you have in common.

Pass the bag to the person on your right. Let him choose an item and take a guess as to what it represents. Continue passing the bag around the circle until

trade secret

If you really want to drive the point home, ask for two volunteers from the group to perform an impromptu skit in which one of them tries to carry on a conversation with the other, who gives only one-word responses.

all of the items have been chosen. Use the following information to guide your discussion of each object.

- *House*—This represents a person's home. Find out where he lives (perhaps general area rather than a specific address), how long he's lived there, where else he's lived, and where he'd like to live in the future.

- *School book*—This represents school. Find out what her favorite and least favorite classes are, who her favorite and least favorite teachers are, what kind of extracurricular activities she's involved in, and how much time she spends doing homework every night.

- *Paycheck stub*—This represents the person's job. Find out where he works, how he likes the job, and where he's worked before.

- *Road map*—This represents the person's travel experiences. How many different states or countries has she visited? What's her favorite area of the country or tourist attraction? If she could live anywhere in the world, where would it be?

  CD / Hacky Sack
- *Fishing pole*—This represents the person's hobbies and interests. Find out what he likes to do in his free time, how he got interested in those activities, and why he enjoys them.

- *Light bulb*—This is a tough one to guess. The light bulb represents the person's ideas or beliefs. What does she feel strongly about? What things have influenced her way of looking at the world?

  Pamphlet
- *College application*—This represents the person's goals or future plans. Where does he see himself five, 10, 20 years from now?

After all of the items have been pulled from the bag, display them someplace in the room where everyone can see them.

For the second part of the activity, assign each person in the group a conversation partner. If you have an odd number of kids, include yourself in the activity. The members of each pair will decide who will be the conversation starter and who will be the responder.

As you may guess from the name, the conversation starter is responsible for starting a conversation with his partner using one or more of the eight topics represented by the items in the bag. If kids forget the topics, they can look at the items to remind them. (If they forget what the items represent, they can ask you.)

Give the pairs two or three minutes to carry on their conversations. When they're finished, have the partners switch roles and try again. After two or three more minutes, bring the group back together.

Discuss the activity using questions like these—

- **How much did the items from the bag help you remember things to talk about?**
- **If you didn't have those reminders, how well do you think you would have done in keeping the conversation going?**
- **What's the hardest part about starting a conversation?**
- **What's the hardest part about keeping a conversation going?**
- **Generally, on a scale of one to 10 (one means "I lag," 10 means "I rip!") how good are you at communicating?**

trade secret
Keep your ears open during this activity and you may discover some things about your group members that will help you connect with them later. Even seemingly insignificant details may turn out to be important. If you don't trust your memory, jot down some notes.

Finish the— 7 min

To personalize your discussion a little more, ask your group members to complete the following sentences. Encourage them to consider their answers carefully before they respond. Start things off by finishing the first statement yourself. Then ask the person on your right to go next. After everyone has responded (or said, "I pass"), move on to the second statement. Continue until all four sentences have been completed.

- **I have a lot of trouble talking with—**
- **I am more of a talker (or listener) because—**
- **The kind of communication that encourages me is—**
- **I really listen closely to [person's name] because—**

The eyes have it 5 min

This next activity is designed to encourage maximum eye contact among your group members. Not everyone will be comfortable with it at first, but if you keep things positive and nonthreatening most kids will probably warm up to the idea.

Here's how you might explain the activity.

Everyone pair up with a person next to you. This exercise may be a little awkward and difficult for some of you, but that's okay. After all, our small group time is supposed to be challenging. Here's what you have to do. Look into your partner's eyes for 30 seconds without saying anything or laughing. And remember this: it's not a stare out, it's a learning experience. While you're staring, try to remember what you're thinking and feeling. Ready? Go!

The beauty of being a hands-on group leader is that you get to enjoy this exercise with your kids. Of course, while you're staring into your partner's eyes, you'll also need to keep track of the time.

When the 30 seconds are over, discuss questions like these as a group.

- **How did you feel during our little eye exercise?**
- **What do you think your partner was thinking during the exercise?**
- **What were you thinking?**
- **How often do you look directly into people's eyes when you talk to them?**
- **How important do you think it is to maintain good eye contact with people when you talk to them? Why?**
- **What can you do to make sure you maintain eye contact during conversations?**

Says you *5 min*

Learning how to have meaningful conversations with people takes work. It's not something that comes naturally to most people. Today we looked at two important parts of conversation: knowing what to talk about and looking people in the eye when you speak. We're not done learning how to be good communicators, though. We've got all kinds of tips and hints to talk about in the next few weeks.

But right now I'd like to take just a few minutes to talk about a different kind of communication. It's one thing to have personal encounters with other people; it's another thing to have a personal encounter with God himself. We may not be able to see God physically, but we can know for sure that he's looking at us. And if we follow his son, Jesus, we can know for sure that he's pleased with us.

Read 2 Corinthians 5:21. (*The Living Bible* communicates this word picture especially well).

That's a great picture of what God does for people who commit their lives to Jesus. I love this picture and what it says about my relationship with God.

Give your kids a chance to respond to the verse or to ask questions.

Did you hear that? *10 min*

As you wrap up this session, try the listening activity you used in your earlier meetings, but this time with a twist. Choose one person from the group to focus on at a time. You and a few of your group members should identify one thing you think the person values and explain why you believe it.

To start the exercise, choose one person from the group and say something like this—

Omar, I think you value your relationship with your father because of the respectful way you talk about him.

After a couple of other people have followed your lead, choose another person in the group to focus on. Continue until everyone has had a turn in the spotlight.

trade secret
Think of this section as an outline, not a script. Cut the parts that don't convey what you want to say, and add your own ideas. In other words, do what you think will work best for your group.

For God took the sinless Christ and poured into him our sins. Then, in exchange, he poured God's goodness into us!
—2 Corinthians 5:21 (*Living Bible*)

trade secret
Don't let your youth ministry end when your meeting does. Schedule some time this week to talk with your kids individually. Consider meeting at a fast-food restaurant or another place where your kids will feel comfortable talking.

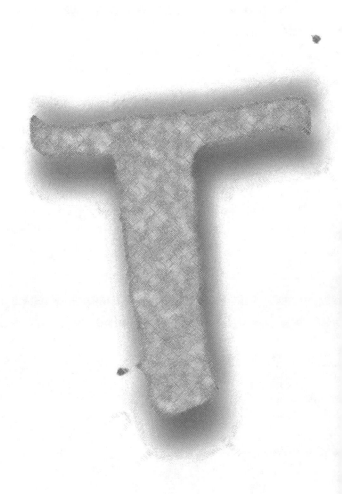

SAYING without SPEAKING

The purpose of this meeting is to help your group members understand the importance of nonverbal forms of communication.

In the beginning *17 min*

Kick off your meeting with an explanation similar to the following:

Our goal for this meeting is to figure out some ways we can become closer as a group. Obviously, communication is one of the most important parts of the relationship-building process. That's why we're going to be focusing our attention on some communication exercises.

For this meeting you'll need...
- A Bible

Some of you may find that this meeting is a real challenge. That's good! Challenges help us grow and learn. Today we'll start with a challenge called Party Time.

Let's have everyone stand up and start milling around like you're at a party. When I say, "Talk," I want you to find a partner and start a conversation on the topic I give you. If I say, "Baseball," you talk about baseball. If I say, "Movies," you talk about movies. If I say, "Schedule B Tax Forms," you talk about interest and dividend income from seller-financed mortgages.

Keep the conversation going until I say, "Switch." Then you'll find a new partner and discuss a different topic, which I'll give you. Here's your first topic: If your bedroom were on fire, what three things would you carry out first and why? Remember to listen when the other person is talking. Go!

If you have an uneven number of group members, join the party yourself. After about two minutes, give the signal to switch. Make sure everyone changes partners; then announce the new topic. Continue the activity for several rounds.

Here are some topics to get you started.

trade secret
If you have the time to come up with topics of your own, all the better. After all, who knows the interests of your group better than you?

- **Describe an important friendship in your life right now.**
- **Describe an important decision you've made in the last year.**
- **Describe why your family is important to you.**
- **Describe ways in which you see yourself changing.**
- **Describe some important traditions in your family.**
- **Name some things you worry about a lot that really aren't very important.**

The perfect greeting *8 min*

Make the transition to your next activity by saying something like this—

You're pretty good at verbal communication. How good are you at nonverbal communication? Whether you know it or not, you're probably communicating nonverbally right now. Nonverbal forms of communication are just as important as verbal ones when it comes to letting people know how we feel. If you don't believe it, check out this demonstration.

You'll need one volunteer to help you with this activity.

Let's say [name your volunteer] and I are in a school hallway. I'm going to greet [your volunteer] several different ways. Each time, though, I'm just going to say one word, "Hi." Notice how the situation changes as I change my nonverbal communication.

You and your volunteer will run through the same scene seven different times. Each time, you will walk up to the person and say, "Hi," altering your nonverbal communication according to the following instructions.

1. Walk past the person, looking continually at the floor, and say, "Hi."
2. Walk past the person, look quickly at him, then down again, and say, "Hi."
3. Walk past the person, look up at him, smile, and say, "Hi."
4. Walk up to the person, stop, look at him, smile, pat him on the arm, and say, "Hi."
5. Walk up to the person, stop, look at him, smile, put your arm on his shoulder (or shake hands), and say, "Hi."
6. Walk up to the person, stop, look at him, smile, give him a sideways hug, and say, "Hi."
7. Announce—but don't demonstrate—that the next step might be a bear hug or a kiss.

After you've gone through the different scenarios, get some feedback from your volunteer. Ask questions like these—

- **Which greetings did you prefer? Why?**
- **Which greetings made you uncomfortable? Why?**
- **How do you think you'd respond if someone greeted you like I did in the last few scenarios?**

After the volunteer shares his feelings, share some of your own thoughts, feelings, and preferences concerning nonverbal communication.

Introduce the next part of your meeting, perhaps by saying —

Let's spend the rest of our time focusing on nonverbal communication. It's not just the way we greet people; it's how we look when we say something, how we stand or sit, and how we hold our bodies. The fact is, we communicate more nonverbally than we do verbally.

Include your group members in the discussion by encouraging them to answer the following questions. If you find that some of your kids are reluctant to respond, call on them specifically. Make this a group-wide discussion.

- **Give me an example of one nonverbal form of communication you've noticed in this meeting so far.**

Be prepared to share an example or two that you've noticed to give your kids an idea of what you're looking for. For instance, did anyone look at his watch or shift in his chair? Both of those actions could be considered nonverbal messages of impatience.

- **Do your parents ever communicate nonverbally? If so, when and how? What are they saying?**
- **Give an example of your own form of nonverbal communication, using only your face or body.**

Give your kids some practice in communicating nonverbally. Explain the activity:

I want each of you to think of an attitude or emotion. One at a time, we're going to try to express those attitudes without using words.

Put yourself on the spot by going first. Convey an attitude such as boredom, disinterest, anger, or love using facial expressions, body language—anything but verbal cues. Let your group members try to guess what emotion you're expressing. After someone correctly guesses what you're trying to communicate, have the person sitting on your right go next. Continue around the circle until everyone has had a chance to express herself nonverbally.

trade secret

Not every exercise or activity in the meeting is going to work with *your* group. Don't let these little failures throw you. Keep your focus on the big picture of the meeting. If you sense that an activity's failing, bail out of it and move on.

You don't say *15 min*

Ask for a volunteer to stand with you in the middle of the circle. Describe the activity by saying something like this—

> **We all have a personal comfort zone. A comfort zone is the amount of space we need around us in order to feel at ease. We're going to do a little experiment now to see how big [the name of your volunteer]'s personal comfort zone is.**

Stand facing your volunteer from a distance. Look him in the eye and smile.

> **I'm going to keep stepping closer and closer to you until you decide I've invaded your personal comfort zone. When that happens, when you start to feel uncomfortable about how close I am, just say, "Stop."**

Take one step toward your volunteer and ask if he's comfortable. If he says, "Yes," take another step. As you get closer, watch for any nonverbal clues the volunteer may give off to indicate growing discomfort. For example, the volunteer may get an embarrassed look on his face, start to lean back, shift his weight to his heels, change the position of his arms, or turn away from you.

Point out any nonverbal clues you pick up on. When the volunteer says, "Stop," give the rest of the group a chance to look at the space between you. Ask other students to explain whether their personal comfort zones are bigger or smaller than your volunteer's.

If you have a few extra minutes, do a little experimenting with body position. Turn away from your volunteer and see whether that makes him feel more comfortable. Stand to his side and see if he still feels uncomfortable. Discuss as a group how a person's comfort zone can change.

Discuss your group members' personal preferences using some of the following questions.

> - **How do you usually greet the people you're closest to?**
> - **What kind of greeting are you most comfortable with?**
> - **What nonverbal forms of communication does your family use?**
> - **Would you describe yourself as a physical person? If so, why do you suppose you're like that? If not, why not?**

trade secret

As you're moving toward your volunteer, give your kids a running commentary as to your own comfort level. When you get too close for comfort, tell your group members about it and explain how you feel.

It's a group thing *15 min*

Prepare your group members for another potentially uncomfortable exercise.

> **It's time for another big challenge. Here's what we're going to do. Without saying a word, we're all going to stand up and greet each other, letting our nonverbal communication do the talking. You might give some people a bear hug, some people a playful punch in the arm,**

some people a high five, and some people a handshake. The only rule is that you have to greet everyone in the group. Ready? Nonverbally communicate!

Afterward, discuss the exercise using questions like the ones below. Ask three or so group members to answer each question.

- **How uncomfortable were you during this activity?**
- **What was uncomfortable about the experience?**
- **How did different people in the group greet you?**
- **Why do you suppose different people were greeted differently?**
- **What's one thing you learned about yourself during this activity?**

Says you *5 min*

Wrap up this meeting by sharing a few thoughts from God's Word.

This session has been a real learning experience for me. I'm still not totally comfortable with all of this nonverbal communication stuff. I have a lot to learn. I just want to thank you for being open to trying these new ideas and activities.

As you've probably noticed by now, each week I try to bring up a Bible verse that relates to our session topic. This week I want to talk about the ways in which God communicates to us.

The Bible tells us that God communicates to us in three different ways: (1) through his son, Jesus Christ; (2) through his book, the Bible; and (3) nonverbally, through his creation.

Read Romans 1:19-20. Then continue.

I can really identify with these verses. When I'm on the beach or in the mountains or just out looking at the stars at night, I can pick up God's nonverbal communication. I see what he's done, and I understand more about him because of it.

Give a personal example of a time God's creation revealed something about him to you.

This has been the second of three lessons on communication. If I could communicate just one thing for you to remember after you leave here today, I'd want you to know that—

Finish this sentence by sharing something personal (and brief) about your faith and your life.

trade secret
Make sure you keep your talk to five minutes or less. Any longer than that, and you risk losing your kids' attention.

Since what may be known about God is plain to them, because God has made it plain to them. For since the creation of the world God's invisible qualities—his eternal power and divine nature—have been clearly seen, being understood from what has been made, so that men are without excuse.

—Romans 1:19-20

trade secret
After the meeting, make it a point to seek out your group members individually to thank them for coming and let them know how glad you are that they came.

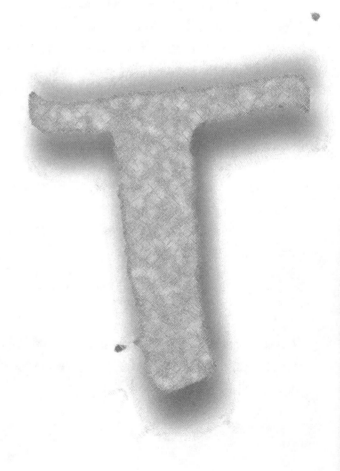

affirm FOUNDATION

The purpose of this meeting is to give your group members a chance to give and receive compliments.

In the beginning *5 min*

At the end of your second meeting, you asked your group members to make a three-week commitment to attend these sessions. This meeting marks the end of that commitment period. When this session ends, you and your kids will decide whether you want to continue meeting together. If so, you'll ask your group members to make another commitment to the group.

> **For this meeting you'll need...**
> • A Bible

Take a few minutes at the beginning of this session to share your personal feelings about the group. Talk about how you've grown as a result of your experiences with the group and how you've come to feel about your group members.

What you *don't* want to do is emotionally blackmail your kids into renewing their commitment to the group. Just because the group is important to *you* doesn't mean it should be important to them. If some of your kids really don't want to commit to the group, they shouldn't feel like they're letting you down. So don't go overboard in sharing your feelings. Be honest but not mushy.

Let your kids know how you see the group progressing from this point on. Tell them about some of the hopes you have for it. At the same time, let your kids know that there will be no hard feelings toward anyone who wants to leave. You asked for a three-week commitment, and (presumably) your kids fulfilled it. They should be able to leave the group with clear consciences, if that's what they decide to do.

If this does turn out to be your last meeting, make sure you end your group time the way you began it—with complete openness and honesty. Remind your group members that no one has to answer any questions during the meeting, but those who do must answer them honestly.

trade secret

If you and your group members continue meeting together, remember this can't-miss axiom:

Informal is better.

Whether it's a discussion, a seating arrangement, or a meeting plan, the less structure you impose, the better your kids will like it.

Finish the— *12 min*

Start this section with comments like these—

Okay, our first activity today is called Finish the Sentence. If you've been to any of our first four meetings, you probably know how this works. If you don't, just remind yourself that the name of the activity is Finish the Sentence. I'll start a sentence, and you finish it. If you don't want to respond, just say, "I pass." If you do feel like answering, be honest.

Go through the sentences one at a time, giving each person a chance to respond to the first one before moving on to the second one. To give your kids an idea of what you're looking for, finish the first couple of sentences yourself before asking your kids to follow suit. After that, let kids answer on a random basis.

- **The most stressful area of my life right now is—**
- **One area of my life in which I'm feeling guilty right now is—**
- **One thing I don't understand about the opposite sex is—**
- **One habit I'm working on changing is—**
- **One area of my life in which I feel really strong and good right now is—**
- **One of the best compliments I've received lately is—**

My compliments *30 min*

Some of you are going to find this session to be a nice change of pace—especially if you've heard lots of insults and put-downs. Today we're going to talk about compliments. Actually, we're going to do more than talk about compliments; we're going to give and receive them!

Find out how your group members feel about compliments by throwing out several questions.

- **What are the best kind of compliments?**
- **How hard is it for you to give sincere compliments? Why?**
- **What's the best way to respond to a compliment?**
- **How hard is it for you to take a compliment? Why?**
- **Which is more difficult for you: giving compliments or receiving them? Why?**

After several group members have responded to these questions, move on to an exercise in which your kids will take turns complimenting each other. Choose one person in the group to focus on at a time. With you leading the way, everyone in the group will give that student a compliment. Then move on to the next person. When the exercise is finished, every person in your group will have been complimented by every other person.

To keep your group members from taking the easy way out or making a joke of this activity, give them a few guidelines for their compliments. Use any or all of the following ideas, and feel free to add some of your own.

- **The compliment should be sincere. It should come straight from your heart.**
- **The compliment should be original. It shouldn't be a repeat of something someone else said.**
- **When you give your compliment, you should look at and talk directly to the person you're complimenting.**

As for the people receiving compliments, suggest that the two best ways to respond are with a smile or a simple *thank you*.

Start the exercise by choosing the first person and offering your own heartfelt compliment. Give the group members a minute or so to think of their own compliments. On average, you'll probably spend three to five minutes on each person.

Outwardly, most of your kids will probably respond to this activity with embarrassed grins or eye rolls. Inwardly, though, they may be doing cartwheels and smiling from ear to ear. Don't underestimate just how inspiring or uplifting this activity can be. Don't rush through it!

Arrange the activity so that you are the last one in the group to be complimented.

High praise indeed *8 min*

Make the transition from the compliment-fest to the Bible study portion of your meeting by asking your kids a few questions.

- **Do you suppose God enjoys being complimented as much as we do? Why or why not?**
- **Have you ever heard God get complimented?**
- **Have you ever complimented him yourself? If so, when? If not, why not?**

If no one else mentions it, point out that there are hundreds of verses in the Bible that compliment God. Some people may call it *praise* or *worship*, but it's really just complimenting him for who he is and what he's done.

Read Psalm 117. Then ask something like—

What if Jesus had been physically sitting in our group during our compliment exercise? What would you have said to him? How would you have complimented the Lord?

Praise the Lord, all you nations; extol him, all you peoples. For great is his love toward us, and the faithfulness of the Lord endures forever. Praise the Lord.

—Psalm 117:1-2

Rather than having your kids *think* about their compliments, ask them to demonstrate their responses by visualizing Jesus sitting in an empty chair in the room—place one in your circle—and offering him a compliment.

You could start the proceedings by looking at the empty chair and saying something like this—

Jesus, one thing that I especially appreciate about you is the way you spent your time on earth with the people who needed you most.

Encourage group members to offer their own compliments to the Lord. Some may respond more than once; others may not share at all.

Where do we go from here? *7 min*

As you wrap up the session, get your kids' responses to these two questions.

- **What did you think was the hardest part of this meeting?**
- **Which compliment surprised you the most or meant the most to you?**

At the end of your meeting, announce that the three-week commitment your group members made at the end of Session 2 has been fulfilled. Thank those who stuck to their commitment for their faithfulness. Take a poll among your group members to see how many of them would like to continue meeting together. Ask those who express an interest to make another three- to five-week commitment.

As for those who choose not to continue, send them away from the meeting with your blessing and your understanding.

FACING life's TENSIONS

The purpose of this meeting is to help your group members talk about the tension they feel about not living up to expectations.

So many questions, so little time *10 min*

If you're a pack rat, you should be all set for the opening activity of this meeting, because you need to dig out the **Question Time** slips that you used during earlier meetings. (Of course, if you didn't save them, cut apart another copy of the sheet.) While you're at it, you'll also need to cut several blank sheets of paper into small slips. You'll use these slips in the second half of the activity.

Hand out three of the **Question Time** slips (randomly) to each group member. Instruct your kids to choose one of their three questions to answer in front of the group. As usual, you should go first, and then continue around the circle.

For this meeting you'll need...

- **Question Time** slips, (pages 21-23), used during previous meetings
- Blank slips of paper
- Pencils
- Copies of **Living in Tension**, (page 51)
- 3 Bibles each marked with one of the following: 1 Samuel 16:7, Matthew 10:29-31, Colossians 1:21-22

So many questions, so little time, part 2 *10 min*

After everyone has answered a question, hand out three to five blank slips of paper to each person along with a pencil. Then say something like—

Using the questions you just answered as models, I want you to write some questions of your own. But when you're writing your questions, I want you to address them either to one specific person in the group or to the entire group. Write the name of the person or just write GROUP

on one side of the slip and your question on the other side. Try to come up with at least three questions. If you're feeling really curious, write five.

Don't just sit back and watch your kids work. Grab a pencil and some slips of paper and write your own questions. Address some to individuals and some to the entire group. After five minutes or so, collect the papers and pencils. First, read the questions that are addressed to specific individuals. Remind your group members that no one has to answer a question. They are free to say, "I pass," to any questions they're not comfortable answering.

After you've gone through the personal questions, read the ones that are addressed to the entire group. Encourage several members to offer their input in answering the questions.

trade secret
Use your best judgment about whether you need to give your kids some parameters for writing questions. For example, would it be a good idea to remind your group members not to write anything insulting or offensive? Sometimes it's better to be safe than sorry in these situations.

Past, present, and future tense *15 min*

Introduce this section with words like these—

> **Now that we're all in a sharing mood, let's talk about today's topic: stress. How many of you have experienced stress or tension this week?**

Unless someone in your group had a really, really good week, you'll probably see all of your kids raise their hands. Ask them what kinds of things cause stress or tension in their lives. Encourage several group members to respond.

If no one else mentions it, guide the discussion to the specific kind of tension you're going to be talking about in today's meeting. Here are some questions you might use to make the transition.

- **Do you act the same way around your friends that you act around your parents? If not, why not? What would happen if you did?**
- **Your parents probably have some expectations for you and your life. What are some of them?**
- **Your friends probably have certain expectations for you and your life, too. What are some of them?**
- **What expectations do you have for your life?**
- **Do you ever feel pressured to live up to the expectations of your family or friends? If so, why do you suppose that is?**
- **Do you ever feel pressured to live up to your own expectations?**
- **How do you feel when you compare the person you are right now with the person you want to be?**

If group members are hesitant to respond to the last question, share an example from your own life of the distance between who you are and who you want to be. For example, if the following description fits you, you might say something like this—

I would like to be someone who is physically fit, who eats right, and who exercises regularly. That's the person I'd like to be. The tension in my life comes from the fact that in reality I struggle with my weight, I eat junk food, and I don't exercise often enough. Because of the difference between who I am and who I want to be, it's easy for me to get down on myself and even quit trying.

It's also easy to get down when I start comparing who I am with who my friends want me to be or who God wants me to be. I don't want to speak for you, but I'm guessing that I'm probably not the only person in this room who struggles with those kinds of feelings. I can't think of a better place for us to talk about those feelings than in this group. Let's give it a try.

Living in tension *20 min*

Hand out copies of **Living in Tension** (page 51) and introduce it by saying something similar to this—

You'll notice that this sheet has several different areas of our lives listed. Let's go through these areas one at a time and talk about how we really are, how we would like to be, how our friends would like us to be, and how God would like us to be.

Begin your discussion with the physical category. Choose one of the topics listed under the category to talk about. For example, if you choose "My athletic abilities," you would talk about how athletic you really are, how athletic you would like to be, how athletic your friends would like you to be, and how athletic God would like you to be.

After you're finished sharing, ask the person on your right to choose one of the five topics to talk about. Continue around the circle until everyone has had a chance to share about a physical area.

Repeat the process with the mental, social, and spiritual categories.

Watch your time carefully during this activity. Conclude your discussion roughly 10 minutes before the meeting is scheduled to end. You may not get through all four categories, but that's okay. Your goal is simply to get your group members talking about who they want to be, who they are, who they think their friends want them to be, and who they think God wants them to be.

Says you *5 min*

Spend a few minutes (but no more than five) helping your kids discover what God's Word has to say about the tension between who we are and who we're expected to be. Adapt the following comments to fit your group and your own personal experiences.

trade secret
If you really want to grab your kids' attention during your brief talk, use some examples based on the things your group members shared in the previous activity.

I don't know about you, but it's sometimes hard for me to admit that I'm not the person I want to be or who my friends want me to be or especially who God wants me to be. Sometimes it's hard for me to even picture the person God wants me to be.

Fortunately for me and others like me—who sometimes forget how God sees us—there are plenty of Bible verses we can turn to for answers. We're going to take a look at three of them right now.

Ask for three volunteers to read the Bible verses. You may want to give each volunteer a Bible with one of the following verses clearly marked for easy reading: 1 Samuel 16:7, Matthew 10:29-31, and Colossians 1:21-22.

After each verse is read, ask for student volunteers to explain what the passage says about the way God sees us.

If you have a few moments at the end of this discussion, share some personal thoughts about positive self-image, considering the fact that God loves us and values us as special and unique people. Wrap up the discussion by saying something like this—

Just as God sees each of us as being special, I see each of you as being special. We're all very different, but each of us has unique strengths and weaknesses. What's more, I think our strengths and weaknesses complement each other nicely. I think we're a good fit as a group.

But the Lord said to Samuel, "Do not consider his appearance or his height, for I have rejected him. The Lord does not look at the things man looks at. Man looks at the outward appearance, but the Lord looks at the heart."

—1 Samuel 16:7

Are not two sparrows sold for a penny? Yet not one of them will fall to the ground apart from the will of your Father. And even the very hairs of your head are all numbered. So don't be afraid; you are worth more than many sparrows.

—Matthew 10:29-31

Once you were alienated from God and were enemies in your minds because of your evil behavior. But now he has reconciled you by Christ's physical body through death to present you holy in his sight, without blemish and free from accusation.

—Colossians 1:21-22

Opening up *10 min*

As we wrap up this meeting, let's do a little personal sharing. Here's the way this will work. I'm going to share with [name the person on your right] one area of strength and one area of struggle I've recognized in my life as a result of this meeting. When I finish, I want the rest of you to do the same, one at a time, with the person on your right. I'd like the entire group to be able to hear what you say. We've got a group here who truly cares about each other, so we should take advantage of it.

After the entire group has shared, close the meeting by thanking the kids for being honest and participating in the meeting.

trade secret

Small group ministry involves more than meeting once a week as a group. Look for opportunities to help, encourage, and challenge your group members outside of your regularly scheduled meetings.

Living in Tension
between who i want to be and who i am

- **The person I am**
- **The person I want to be**
- **The person my friends want me to be**
- **The person God wants me to be**

Physical
- My athletic abilities
- My partying habits
- My sexual life
- My physical fitness
- My appearance

Social
- The way I act as a friend
- The way I act as a boyfriend or girlfriend
- The way I act as a daughter or son
- The way I act as a date

Mental
- My study methods
- My favorite movies and TV shows
- My daydreams
- My goals and future plans

Spiritual
- My time with God
- My attitude about God around my friends
- My personal thoughts about God each day
- My feelings of forgiveness
- My Bible study time and prayer

Living in Tension
between who i want to be and who i am

- **The person I am**
- **The person I want to be**
- **The person my friends want me to be**
- **The person God wants me to be**

Physical
- My athletic abilities
- My partying habits
- My sexual life
- My physical fitness
- My appearance

Social
- The way I act as a friend
- The way I act as a boyfriend or girlfriend
- The way I act as a daughter or son
- The way I act as a date

Mental
- My study methods
- My favorite movies and TV shows
- My daydreams
- My goals and future plans

Spiritual
- My time with God
- My attitude about God around my friends
- My personal thoughts about God each day
- My feelings of forgiveness
- My Bible study time and prayer

what's IMPORTANT

The purpose of this meeting is to help your group members identify what's important to them.

In the beginning *5 min*

Gather the group members together in a circle, either on the floor or on chairs around a table. Adapt the following introductory comments so they reflect your own personal experiences. Get a few responses from your kids to the questions before continuing.

If someone were to ask you what's important in your life, what would you say? If that same person were to take a look at the way you live, do you think he'd be able to spot those things you consider important?

I don't know about you, but sometimes I say something is important to me but then live my life as though it's not. For example, when I was in high school, if you'd have asked what was important in my life, I probably would have said my grades. I knew that grades were important to my future, but I didn't act as though they were. I blew off assignments, didn't study as well as I should have, and goofed around in class. So do you think grades were really important to me?

Another example is saving money. If you were to ask me, I'd say saving money is important to me. Someday I'd like to have enough money to live comfortably after I retire. But if you see me out spending my paychecks on clothes, skis, junk food, and other things, you might

trade secret

In a small group setting, enthusiasm is usually contagious. If you approach this meeting with excitement, chances are at least some of your kids will as well.

For this meeting you'll need...

- Pipe cleaners, 5 per student, a different color for each person
- A piece of thick Styrofoam or slab of clay
- A camera (optional)
- Table (optional)
- Bibles

not believe that saving money is important to me.

What I'm trying to say is that when it comes to what's important in our lives, what we say and how we live don't always match up. Enough about me, though. Let's talk about what's important to you.

Finish the— *10 min*

Rather than putting your kids on the spot by asking them to name the important things in their lives, let them complete the following sentences. Let them deal with one area at a time. Explain that you'll start the sentence, and your kids can call out their answers whenever they're ready.

- **One important thing my family does together is—**
- **One important belief I have about life is—**
- **One important habit I want to continue is—**
- **One important decision I need to make is—**

Piped in *30 min*

You may want to pull up to a table for this activity. Give each group member five pipe cleaners of the same color. Make sure, though, that each person is given a unique color. So if you have eight people in the group, you'll need eight different colors of pipe cleaners. Place some kind of base in the center of the circle. A piece of thick Styrofoam or a slab of clay will probably work best, but anything that pipe cleaners can be stuck into will do. Then make comments like these—

Since chances are none of you smokes a pipe, you're probably wondering what these pipe cleaners are for. The answer is, an art project. We're going to use each pipe cleaner to make a symbol of something that's important to us.

Here's how it will work. I'll ask you five questions. You'll respond to each one by bending and twisting one of your pipe cleaners into a certain shape or symbol. After we've gone through all five questions, we'll display our pipe cleaners and explain what they stand for. Then we'll stick them into the base.

When we're all done, we'll have a unique sculpture that represents what's important to each of us and to our group. It will be a one-of-a-kind piece of art. Nowhere on earth will there be another sculpture like this one.

Here's the first question. Your challenge is to make—using one pipe cleaner—a symbol that represents your answer. Don't worry about hurrying your answer. I'll give you plenty of time to make your symbol.

Use these questions or ones like them.

1. **Who is one of the most important people in your life?**
2. **What is one important mistake that you've made and now want to avoid repeating?**
3. **What is one of the most important goals in your future?**
4. **What is one of the most important beliefs that you hold?**
5. **What is one of the most important things about you that you haven't yet told us as a small group?**

Remind your group members that if any of them don't want to answer a question, they can simply say, "I pass."

After you've gone through all five questions and given your kids time to create five different pipe cleaner symbols, begin your discussion of the activity.

Who's brave enough to start things off by showing us your response to the first question?

When you get a volunteer, ask her to let you guess what her piece of work represents before she reveals the answer.

After a few kids have made their guesses, ask your volunteer to explain her work and then stick the pipe cleaner into the base. Continue with the first question until everyone has shared and placed her symbol on the base. Then move on to the next question. Continue until all five questions have been answered.

Says you *5 min*

Introduce the Bible study portion of the meeting with words like these—

You know, our little sculpture here isn't the only unique thing in this room. Can you find any other things that are one of a kind?

If no one mentions that everyone in the room is unique, let your group members discover it through God's word by saying something like—

I want to read five verses that King David wrote in the book of Psalms. We can't say for sure what David was feeling when he wrote these words, but it's possible that he was just beginning to understand how special he really was and how God had created him as a completely unique person.

Read Psalm 139:14-16 and 23-24.

God looks at the sculpture of our lives and loves each of us exactly as we are. In fact, he proved his love for us by sending his son to suffer

the punishment for our sins! I can honestly tell you that my faith in God is the most important thing in my life. But I hope I don't have to tell you that; I hope you can see it in my life—the way I live, the things I do and don't do. I would like to pray and thank God for our time together and for you.

Before you wrap up your meeting, lead your kids in a brief prayer, thanking God for your group members and the time you spend together each week.

Did you hear that? *8 min*

I'd like us to end our meeting with two quick activities. First, I'd like each of us to finish this sentence: One thing I will remember about this meeting is—

You should finish the sentence first and then encourage the rest of your group members to take a turn.

Second, as we leave today, I'd like each of us to encourage at least three other people. That might mean giving someone a hug, saying something meaningful, or doing whatever else you want to do to offer encouragement.

Let the kids mingle on the way out the door.

trade secret

Be sure to let your group members know that you also pray for them outside your meeting time. (If you haven't been, you can start now!) Let them know not only that you're thinking about them throughout the week, but that you believe your prayers can impact their lives.

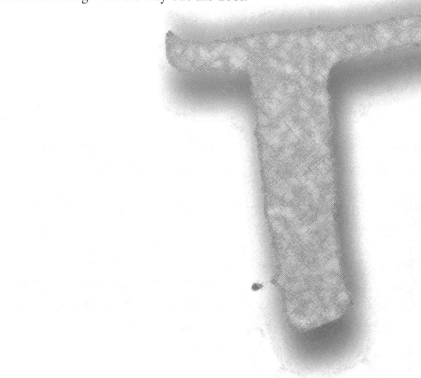

SPY

The purpose of this meeting is to help your group members make honest observations about themselves and their lives.

In the beginning *1 min*

The topic of this meeting is observations, so it might be a good idea to make sure you and your kids have similar ideas about what the word means. Ask them to explain what an observation is. If your kids have some trouble coming up with one specific definition, suggest one like this—

> **For this meeting you'll need...**
>
> • Bibles

An observation is an idea or opinion that comes from watching or noticing things.

If you're like most people, you probably make hundreds of observations a day, most of them without even realizing it. All of us make observations about people, places, things—even ourselves.

Basically there are two kinds of observations: the outward kind and the inward kind. Some people are extremely observant when it comes to other people but aren't very observant at all when it comes to the things going on in their own lives. Others are able to focus more on themselves but not as much on other people. Where do you stand? How observant are you? Let's find out.

Physical observations *4 min*

Explain to the kids that now they're going to test their observation skills. Tell them you're going to assign them partners, and they are to sit back to back with their partners so they can't see each other. Pair off the kids and give them a chance to get into position. Then explain in words similar to these—

I'm going to ask you to describe some things about your partner, based on your observations. By the way, from this point on, you're not allowed to look at or talk to your partner at all.

Here are some questions to get you started. Feel free to add or substitute your own questions.

- **Describe your partner's shoes.**
- **Describe your partner's clothing as specifically as you can.**
- **Describe any jewelry your partner is wearing.**
- **Describe your partner's hair and eyes.**

Spend a few minutes at the end of this exercise talking about how observant your group members proved to be. Ask volunteers to talk about why they were or weren't able to answer questions about their partners.

Everyday observations *10 min*

Okay, okay, no more tests. Now tell the kids you'll be spending a few minutes talking about the kinds of things we notice every day. Tell them you'll start a few sentences, and you want them to finish them.

- **On the way to this meeting, I observed—**
- **When I entered this room, I observed—**
- **One observation I made at school, at work, or at home today is—**
- **One recent observation I made about my father or mother is—**
- **One observation I've made about one of my good friends is—**
- **One observation I've made about this group is—**

Compare your group members' responses to see which people tend to make similar observations. If you have a few extra minutes, you might talk about what a person's observations say about him.

Personal observations *15 min*

Transition to this section with comments like these—

Hey, this is an observant group of people! I think we're ready for the next level of observation, the personal level. For some reason, it's harder for most people to notice things that are going on inside them than it is to notice things going on around them. Why do you suppose that is?

Encourage a few of your group members to share their opinions. Then continue with something similar to this—

We're going to spend a few minutes talking about our personal observations, our private responses to things going on in our lives. It might be a little challenging at first, but I think you're up to the challenge. I'm going to start a few more sentences, and I want you to finish them as honestly as you can.

- **One thing I was feeling on my way to this meeting was—**
- **One thing I'm feeling about this school year is—**
- **One thing I'm feeling about a certain member of my family is—**
- **One thing I've noticed about myself since we started meeting together is—**
- **One thing I've noticed about myself when someone in the group starts to get really honest is—**
- **One thing I've noticed about myself when I spend time with someone of the opposite sex is—**

Biblical observations *15 min*

Change the subject a bit with words like these—

Hey, we're on a roll now! I wonder if we could take our observation skills and use them on the Bible. Let's try it. I'll read some Bible verses to you. Listen carefully to what I read and make your own observations. First, think about how the people in the Bible reacted to what they saw and heard. Then think about how you react to the story.

The verses I'm going to read to you describe the things that took place after Jesus was killed on the cross. Jesus' disciples were confused. They expected him to defeat his enemies. They weren't expecting him to die. After his death, they had to figure out what went wrong and what they were going to do. Put yourself in their shoes while you listen to the story.

Read John 20:24-31. Afterward, find out what your group members observed by asking the some questions—

- **Did you notice anything unusual in the story?**
- **What observations did you make about the events going on during this story?**
- **What observations did you make about the feelings of the people involved?**
- **What did you think about Thomas?**

trade secret
You're going to set the tone for this activity. If you're brutally—but responsibly!—honest about yourself, your kids will probably follow your example. Create an environment in your group in which kids feel comfortable sharing even nonflattering things about themselves.

Now Thomas (called Didymus), one of the Twelve, was not with the disciples when Jesus came. So the other disciples told him, "We have seen the Lord!"

But he said to them, "Unless I see the nail marks in his hands and put my finger where the nails were, and put my hand into his side, I will not believe it."

A week later his disciples were in the house again, and Thomas was with them. Though the doors were locked, Jesus came and stood among them and said, "Peace be with you!" Then he said to Thomas, "Put your finger here; see my hands. Reach out your hand and put it into my side. Stop doubting and believe."

Thomas said to him, "My Lord and my God!"

Then Jesus told him, "Because you have seen me, you have believed; blessed are those who have not seen and yet have believed."

Jesus did many other miraculous signs in the presence of his disciples, which are not recorded in this book. But these are written that you may believe that Jesus is the Christ, the Son of God, and that by believing you may have life in his name.

—John 20:24-31

- **What were your own reactions to the story?**
- **Who did you identify with in the story?**

Wrap up your Bible study with a few observations—

Some people think Bible study is boring. Maybe that's because they're not looking closely enough at what they're reading and not making observations about their own feelings or the feelings of others.

Says you *5 min*

This would be a great time for you to share some personal comments about your faith and how doubt has played a role in it. You'll probably find many of your kids nodding in agreement while you talk, because most teenagers struggle with doubt at one point or another.

If you need some direction in what to say, try reading Mark 9:24 to your group and making a few comments on it.

Immediately the boy's father exclaimed, "I do believe; help me overcome my unbelief!"
—Mark 9:24

Final observations *10 min*

Conclude your meeting by asking your kids to share a few observations about your group. Read some of the following sentences, and ask your group members to complete them.

- **One observation I've made about our group is—**
- **One observation I've made about a specific person in the group is—**
- **One observation I've made about our group leader is—**

ALL about ME

The purpose of this meeting is to help your group members look honestly at themselves, their lives, and their relationship with Christ.

Simply stated   *12 min*

Before the meeting you'll need to gather a bagful of miscellaneous items: a $20 bill, a set of keys, a shoe, a piece of jewelry, a Bible, and a candy bar. If you can't round up everything on the list, feel free to make some creative substitutions.

To begin the meeting, place the bag in the middle of your circle. Explain the activity—

> **For this meeting you'll need...**
> • Bag filled with the following items: $20 bill, keys, shoe, piece of jewelry, Bible, and candy bar
> • Bibles

This is a bagful of sentence starters. One at a time, we're going to pull an item from the bag and make a personal statement about it. For example, if I pulled a $20 bill from the bag, I might say something like this—

"I wish I had $20."
"If I had $20, I'd buy ice cream for everybody."
"I once spent $20 on a bootleg CD that turned out to be blank."
You can make any kind of statement you'd like about the object, as long as it's honest and as long as it says something about you. If you want to be profound, be profound. If you want to be simple, be simple. Just make sure you tell the truth.

Pull the first item from the bag, make a short personal statement about it, and pass it to the person on your right. That person should then make a personal statement about it and pass it on. After everyone has made a statement about the first item, pull a second item from the bag and repeat the process. Continue until everyone in the group has commented on each item.

If you have some extra time at the end of this activity (and if your kids are enjoying themselves), continue the proceedings using some things that your kids should pretend are in the bag. These items should include a telephone, a wheelchair, an elderly person, a report card, a bottle of whiskey, and God.

Buddy up   *20 min*

Now that you've had some interesting communication as a group, tell the kids that you're going to move to one-on-one settings. Let them know you're going to assign each kid to a partner, and then you're going to give them a topic to talk about. Tell them that their job is to keep the conversation going until you say, "Switch." When that happens, each group member is to find a different partner and start talking about a different topic, which you will provide.

Assign partners, and then give each pair a minute or so to stake out its own conversation area in the room. If there's an odd number of kids in your group, even things up by becoming someone's partner.

Here are some topics you might suggest for the pairs to talk about.

- **The best and worst things that happened during the week**
- **The best and worst things about school in general**
- **The best and worst things about their families**
- **Future plans**
- **Hidden talents**
- **Secret fears**

Give your kids about four minutes with each of four different partners. Make sure that everyone actually changes partners when it's time and that no one pairs up with the same person more than once during the activity. You'll find that most partners start out talking about their assigned topic, but then move on to other subjects. That's okay. Don't discourage conversation unless you hear kids talking inappropriately.

Finish the—   *10 min*

Bring your group members back together in a circle for the now-familiar exercise of finishing sentences that you read. Encourage your kids to be honest and open in their answers—assuming, of course, that they choose to answer. They always have the option of declining to respond.

Explain that the sentence starters are designed to get your kids talking about themselves. You can use the suggestions provided below or come up with some of your own.

- **I wish I had the courage to—**
- **I get people's attention by—**
- **My greatest strength is—**
- **I get into trouble when I—**
- **The most powerful person I know is—**

- I'm afraid to—
- If someone were to write a book about me, it would be called—
- What really turns me off is—
- I like it when somebody says to me—
- I feel comfortable when—
- When I feel afraid, I—
- When someone laughs at me, I feel—

Picture this 15 min

Open this section of the meeting by saying something like this—

If a picture is worth a thousand words, this next activity could fill the pages of some of your thickest school textbooks. What we're going to do is talk about our personal feelings. But instead of using straightforward sentences like normal people do, we're going to use word pictures to describe how we feel.

You may have no idea what I'm talking about, so I'll give you an example to think about. If you were to describe your life as, say, a boat, you'd have all kinds of word pictures to choose from. You might be anything from a cruise ship to a tugboat, depending on how you feel about yourself. The water you travel through—which could represent the things that are going on in your life—could be anything from a calm lake to raging river rapids. The more details you add to your picture, the easier it will be for the rest of us to figure out how you're doing.

Now that you've given your kids something to think about, let them run with the boat scenario. This might be a tricky activity for some of your less imaginative group members. Make sure you go first to give them an idea of what you're looking for. If you'd like to add some details to the scenario, you might ask kids to describe where Jesus is in their boat and what he's doing. Of course, let a student use a different word picture if she would like.

trade secret

As your group members share their word pictures, look for ways to encourage them to add details to their descriptions. Remember, the more they share, the better the group will get to know them.

Says you 5 min

Tell the kids that so far, they've done a lot of talking about their lives, and it's been great. Then say something like—

I think we've all learned some things about each other that we didn't know before. But we haven't talked much about what I think is the most important part of our lives yet. We haven't talked much about following Jesus and what that means for our everyday existence.

If you have a few extra minutes, find out what some of your group members think following Jesus means and involves. After you've gotten a few responses, help your kids see what the Bible says about it.

Read Luke 14:27-30. Then continue with something like this—

Following Jesus takes some work and some sacrifice. But it's worth it. Jesus made a promise to those who are willing to serve him and pay the cost of following him. Thanks for listening and for being willing to do some honest thinking. I value the friendships we're building in this group. I look forward to these meetings all week.

Give your kids plenty of time to ask questions they may have about Jesus and what it means to follow him.

Did you hear that? *5 min*

So far, you've led your group members through several sharing exercises. As you wrap up the session, try a listening activity. After all, you want your kids to believe the thoughts, feelings, and experiences they share in your meetings are important to the rest of the group.

Lead your kids in a listening check. Choose one person from the group to focus on at a time. You and your group members should then take turns recalling information you learned about the person during the meeting. Ideally, everyone in the group should contribute at least one recollection to the activity. If that doesn't happen, though, don't worry about it.

As usual, you'll probably need to take the lead in this exercise. Choose one person in the group to focus on first. After you start the ball rolling, encourage your kids to recall some new personal information they learned about that person during the meeting. After most of your kids have shared, choose another person in the group to focus on. Continue until everyone has had her turn in the spotlight.

And anyone who does not carry his cross and follow me cannot be my disciple. Suppose one of you wants to build a tower. Will he not first sit down and estimate the cost to see if he has enough money to complete it? For if he lays the foundation and is not able to finish it, everyone who sees it will ridicule him, saying, "This fellow began to build and was not able to finish."

—Luke 14:27-30

trade secret

If time gets tight at the end of your meeting, you may be tempted to skip this section. *Don't.* This activity is important because it helps kids recognize that the others in the group are actually paying attention to them.

the BEAUTY of DIVERSITY

The purpose of this meeting is to help group members recognize and appreciate their differences.

In the beginning *10 min*

Kick off the meeting with an informal time of sharing. You might introduce it this way—

> I'm sure quite a few things have happened in our lives since the last time we got together. With all of our busy schedules, we may miss out on some important events and occurrences in each other's lives if we don't make an effort to connect occasionally. Let's take a few minutes at the beginning of our meeting to get caught up with each other. Let's fill in the group by making three statements about our week. I'll start.

For this meeting you'll need...

- A bag containing some of these items: cotton balls, stapler, scissors, paper cup, eyeglasses, paper clip, pencil with eraser, wadded paper
- Magazines
- Blank sheets of typing paper
- Clear tape
- Bibles
- Copies of I'd Choose You (page 69)

Briefly share three different things that happened to you this week or three different thoughts or revelations you had about your life. When you're finished, ask for a volunteer from the group to do the same. Continue until everyone has had an opportunity to share about the week that was.

What's the difference? *15 min*

Now say that you're going to shift gears a little. Then continue this way—

> **For the past several weeks, we've been focusing on the things we have in common, the interests and experiences we share as members of this group. Today we're going to focus on the many ways in which we're different. To get you thinking along those lines, let's try an activity that calls for a little creative thinking on your part.**

For this activity you'll need a bag filled with at least five or six of the following items: cotton balls, a stapler, scissors, a paper cup, eyeglasses, a paper clip, a pencil with an eraser, and wadded paper. If you can't find everything on the list, make your own creative substitutions.

Place your bag of goodies in the middle of the circle. Explain the exercise by saying something like—

> **One at a time, each of us is going to grab an object from this bag and name one way that we're different from the item. We're not going to settle for obvious differences, though. If you pull out a stapler and say something like, "This is metal, and I'm not," you'll leave us no choice but to boo you mercilessly. Be creative in the differences you look for!**

To give your kids an example of what you're looking for, pull the pencil from the bag and hold it up. Explain one of the differences between you and the writing utensil with words like these—

> **Unlike this pencil, I don't have the equipment to make my mistakes go away. When I botch something, the evidence is usually right out in the open for everyone to see. I can't just go over it a few times and make it disappear. I have to live with the mistakes I make.**

After you've drawn the first item and explained one of your differences, ask the person on your left to draw an item from the bag and come up with a difference. Continue around the circle until everyone has had a chance to share.

Inside and Out *20 min*

> **Okay, let's move on to something a little more challenging. Let's take a look at the differences in our own life, between who we appear to be and who we are.**

Hand out two or three magazines and a blank sheet of paper folded in half to each group member. Make sure that you have several rolls of tape available. Say something like this—

> **This is a two-part exercise. First, go through these magazines and find three to five pictures, phrases, or words that describe your outward**

life, the image you present to people, the way others see you. You can ask yourself this question: if someone followed me around for a week, what would he see?

Give your kids a few minutes to tear out the appropriate pictures or words and tape them on the outside of their folded sheets of paper. Then continue.

Next, find three to five pictures, words, or phrases that describe your inner life, the thoughts and feelings you keep to yourself, the person you are in your heart. Think of some things that, for better or worse, very few people know about you.

Give your kids a few minutes to tear out the second set of pictures or words and tape them on the inside of their folded sheets.

When everyone is finished, display the pictures and words you chose for the outside of your sheet and explain what they represent. One at a time, have the kids briefly explain their choices. After everyone has shared the outside of their sheets, repeat the process with the words and pictures chosen for the inside.

Says you *5 min*

trade secret
This would be a great time to serve your kids some snacks or at least something to drink. Make it an informal time of working and talking.

Have you noticed that we're all very different people? You've probably already spotted dozens of differences just in the short time we've been together today. I don't know about you, but I enjoy the things that set us apart. I certainly wouldn't want everyone to be like me, and I don't think you'd want everyone else to be like you. Can you imagine what a boring world that would be?

I think it's safe to say that God appreciates our differences. After all, he's the one who made us this way. When Jesus walked the earth, he related to many different kinds of people. He cared about them all. He paid attention to everyone.

trade secret
If you can't keep your talk to five minutes, you're trying to do too much. Keep this sharing time short, clear, and practical. Here are some suggestions.

If your students are familiar with the Bible, ask them to call out some of the different people Jesus encountered and helped in the Bible. If no one else mentions them, you might remind your kids of some of the following characters.

- **The boy who had little more to offer than a few loaves of bread and a couple of fish**
- **The leper no one wanted to go near**
- **The woman who was facing a death penalty for having an extramarital affair**
- **The dishonest tax collector who was hated by everyone**
- **The torturer of Christians who eventually ended up writing almost half of the New Testament**

The next time someone tries to convince you that God wants people to look and act the same, remind him of the different people Jesus embraced in the Bible. In fact, here are a few verses you can read to him.

Read John 8:2-11. Then continue.

Jesus loved, cared about, and protected a real person—a prostitute who was caught having an affair with a guy. Jesus' attitude has changed in the past 2,000 years. I believe he loves each of us in this group just as we are. And I believe he wants us to be his followers. He can take the things in our lives that make us different and use them in ways we can't imagine. I believe Jesus loves variety and uses it to carry out his will.

He wants us, as different as we are, to love him, serve him, and give him our lives. I hope that each week you're asking yourself if you're willing to be his—all his. Are you willing to give Jesus everything—even your differences?

Choosers *10 min*

Before you wrap up the meeting, hand out pencils and copies of **I'd Choose You** (page 69). Then say something like this—

Read through the different categories on this sheet and decide which people you would choose from our group to fill them. You can put more than one person's name in a blank, but you have to use each person's name at least once.

Give your kids a few minutes to complete the sheet. When they're finished, give them a few more minutes to share their responses with each other. If you have some extra time at the end of your meeting, ask a few volunteers to explain why they chose certain people for certain categories.

At the end of your meeting, announce that the commitment your group members made at the end of Session 5 has been fulfilled. Thank those who stuck to their commitment for their faithfulness. Take a poll among your group members to see how many of them would like to continue meeting together. Ask those who express an interest to make another commitment for a length of time you all agree on (six weeks, 21 weeks, the number of weeks left until the next big vacation or end of school). Be sure to repeat this process as necessary. As for those who choose not to continue, send them away from the meeting with your blessing and your understanding.

At dawn he appeared again in the temple courts, where all the people gathered around him, and he sat down to teach them. The teachers of the law and the Pharisees brought in a woman caught in adultery. They made her stand before the group and said to Jesus, "Teacher, this woman was caught in the act of adultery. In the Law Moses commanded us to stone such women. Now what do you say?" They were using this question as a trap, in order to have a basis for accusing him.

But Jesus bent down and started to write on the ground with his finger. When they kept on questioning him, he straightened up and said to them, "If any one of you is without sin, let him be the first to throw a stone at her." Again he stooped down and wrote on the ground.

At this, those who heard began to go away one at a time, the older ones first, until only Jesus was left, with the woman still standing there. Jesus straightened up and asked her, "Woman, where are they? Has no one condemned you?"

"No one, sir," she said.

"Then neither do I condemn you," Jesus declared. "Go now and leave your life of sin."

—John 8:2-11

I'd choose you

Fill in each blank below with the name of the group member who you think best fits that category.

I'd choose you—

to be my roommate in college _____

to be with me after the death of
someone in my family _____

to travel around the country
with me for a summer _____

to help me work on my car_____

to help me plan a special birthday celebration _____

to share a very difficult and
private problem with_____

to give me advice about living
my Christian faith _____

to spend an evening with me and my parents _____

to spend a fun and crazy afternoon with me_____

to double-date with me _____

to be my best friend _____

to run my campaign for a student
office in school _____

to recommend to my boss _____

to be on my athletic team_____

to say something at my funeral _____

to buy me a Christmas present _____

to pick a future spouse for me_____

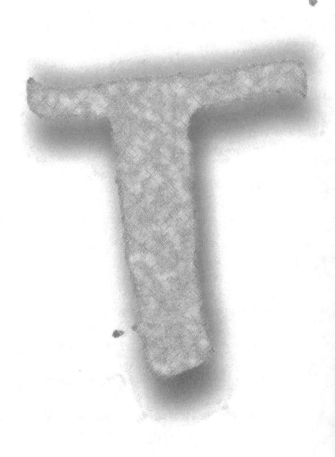

that's WHAT i LIKE about ME

The purpose of this meeting is to help group members understand they have tremendous value.

In the beginning *10 min*

Now give your students a taste of what it's like to try to communicate in the middle of chaos. First, pair them up. Second, distract them! If your group is small, put on a loud CD in the background, or open the door to let in traffic noise, or conduct this activity next door among the preschool class. If your group is larger, have partners at least sit in a circle—and diametrically opposite their partners. Explain the activity this way—

> **For this meeting you'll need...**
>
> - Boom box & CD, or other audio distraction to conversation (optional)
> - Bibles
> - China plate
> - Paper plate

> **All you have to do for the first part of this exercise is talk to your partner. Sounds simple enough, right? Well, it's not. You see, you have to stay in your seats while you talk. And did I mention that everyone in the group will be talking at the same time?**
>
> **I'll give you a few seconds to clean the wax out of your ears, since you're going to have to listen carefully to hear what your partner says. Don't worry about finding something to talk about. I'll be giving you topics to discuss during the activity.**

Here are some topics you might use for the exercise.

- **The good and bad things that happened to you during the past week**
- **An area of your life that's causing stress right now**
- **Your social life**
- **Something you're anticipating or looking forward to**

Announce the topics one at a time and give the partners a minute or so to talk about each one. It's likely that the room will get very loud during this activity, so brace yourself (and anyone who happens to be nearby).

After all four topics have been discussed, get some feedback from your kids. Encourage each group member to share his reactions to and observations about the exercise. Then toss out one more question for your kids to answer—

What can we learn about carrying on conversations in distracting places?

Howdy, partner *10 min*

Comment how well the kids did at communicating, considering the circumstances. Then comment along these lines—

Now let's move on to something a little more difficult. Get together with your partner and find a place to sit. I will give you five activities to do with your partner, none of which will take more than one minute of your time.

Give the pairs the following list of instructions or substitute some of your own ideas—

- **Look into your partner's eyes for 30 seconds.**
- **Give your partner a back rub for 20 seconds.**
- **Give your partner two sincere compliments.**
- **Share with your partner two ways in which you're changing as a person or two things that you've learned about yourself recently.**
- **Share with your partner one honest struggle you're having.**

After the pairs have completed all five instructions, gather the group together to discuss the exercise. Use questions like these to get the discussion rolling—

Were any of these five activities uncomfortable or difficult for you? If so, which ones? What did you learn from this activity that was meaningful to you?

Ask me *25 min*

Prepare your kids for the next exercise by asking some fun questions like these—

- **Have you ever wanted to be a celebrity?**
- **What kind of celebrity would you like to be—a sports hero, a famous actor, a rock star?**

- **How well do you think you'd handle interviews if you were a celebrity? Why?**

After several group members have responded, announce that you'll be giving your kids a chance to be interviewed like real celebrities. One at a time, each person will choose a topic from the list below that seems comfortable to him. Modify the list to suit your group. The rest of the group will then be able to ask the person questions about that topic.

As always, group members should not be forced to answer any question they are uncomfortable with. However, in the spirit of the interview process, the person on the hot seat should be as open, honest, and accommodating as possible.

Here are some topics for your kids to choose from.

- **My self image**
- **My romantic relationship**
- **My ideas about politics**
- **My money habits**
- **My sexual beliefs**
- **My ideas about marriage**
- **My questions about college**
- **My faith in God**

If you have a hard time finding a volunteer to be interviewed first, volunteer for the position yourself. A great topic for you to tackle is *why I lead a small group.*

Allow two to four minutes for the group to grill each interviewee. Make sure that everyone has an opportunity to be questioned.

Says you *5 min*

Introduce this section by reminding the kids that the foundation of your life is your relationship with Jesus. Then continue with words similar to these—

> **You probably also know that I'm not the kind of person who pushes my beliefs on other people. That doesn't mean that I can't share the things that are important to me with my friends. You see, my faith in Jesus helps me understand how important my life is! And since you're my friends, I'd like to tell you about it.**

Hold up a paper plate and a china plate, and say something like this—

> **One thing Jesus has done is help me realize that my life is more like a china plate than a paper plate. Both kinds of plates are useful for the same purpose. Both do the job. Both hold food and allow me to eat. The paper plate, though, is used and then destroyed. Its after-meal value is nothing.**

Demonstrate this point by ripping up the paper plate and throwing the pieces on the floor.

trade secret

While you're on the hot seat, keep in mind that the honesty, openness, and vulnerability you model will set the tone for the rest of your group members. Under the right circumstances, this can be an extremely beneficial activity for a small group.

Sometimes I feel like a paper plate. I feel useless, unimportant, as if my life doesn't matter. I feel like nobody cares. It seems like nothing I do turns out right. I can't reach my goals. I can't make a difference in this complicated world.

Hold up the china plate again.

A china plate is different. It has value even after it's used. We take good care of china and even cherish it. Jesus reminds me that I'm a china-plate person. I have value. I can make a difference.

How can I be sure of my value? All I have to do is remind myself that Jesus died for me. After that, how can I ever consider myself a mere paper-plate person? The value of anything has to do with its cost. Jesus paid his life for mine so I can spend eternity with him. If I believe that, I have to believe that I'm worth something.

Read John 3:16.

There is nothing that can separate us from God's love. Nothing in your past, present, or future can force you away from that kind of love.

Read Romans 8:38-39.

Remember, you and your friends are china-plate people to God. He's your friend. He wants you as his friend, too.

For God so loved the world that he gave his one and only Son, that whoever believes in him shall not perish but have eternal life.
—John 3:16

For I am convinced that neither death nor life, neither angels nor demons, neither the present nor the future, nor any powers, neither height nor depth, nor anything else in all creation, will be able to separate us from the love of God that is in Christ Jesus our Lord.
—Romans 8:38-39

The wrap up *10 min*

Wrap up your meeting by asking your kids to respond to the plate analogy you introduced in the previous section. Use the following questions to guide your discussion.

- When do you most feel like a paper-plate person?
- When do you most feel like a china-plate person?
- What can you do this week to make someone else feel like a valuable, china-plate person?

Encourage several group members to respond to each question. Bring the session to a close with words of encouragement like these—

I think each of you is a special china-plate person. I see great potential in all of you. I hope you'll continue to grow and that you'll spend some time getting to know my friend Jesus—who also happens to think each of you is a china-plate person!

what's IMPORTANT in life

The purpose of this meeting is to help your group members identify their personal priorities and convictions.

In the beginning *10 min*

Start things off with a brief time of sharing. Introduce the exercise along these lines—

> **Has anything happened in your life since the last time we got together? Maybe you took a weekend trip with your family. Maybe you saw a good movie. Maybe you bombed. Whatever happened to you, good or bad, you've got 90 seconds to tell us about it. I'll go first.**

For this meeting you'll need...

- Copies of the **Picture Page** (page 78)
- Bibles

Briefly share the various things that happened to you during the week. When you're finished, ask for a volunteer from the group to do the same. Continue until everyone has had a chance to share.

Little pictures *10 min*

Hand out copies of **Picture Page** (page 78). Give your group members instructions like these—

> **Look closely at the first picture. If you were one of the three people in the picture, which person would you be? What would the hill represent in your life? What would the heavy load be?**

trade secret

Your kids will be trying to relate concrete events in their lives to abstract pictures, a very difficult thing to do. Show them courtesy and understanding by listening intently to what they say, asking questions as necessary.

Give your kids a minute or two to consider the question before asking volunteers to respond. If you find that your group members are hesitant to volunteer answers, call on individuals directly. (But you can also remind your kids they don't have to answer any question they're uncomfortable with.) If you find your kids are a little confused about the kind of responses you're looking for, answer the questions yourself first.

After you've worked out the kinks with the first question, continue your discussion of the **Picture Page** with two more questions.

- **How does the second picture relate to your life this week?**
- **In the third picture, what does the wall represent in your life? What situation or circumstance are you trying to climb over?**

Says you 5 min

trade secret

The comments suggested below are just that—suggestions. For your talk to be effective, it'll have to come from your heart and reflect your true feelings. Filter the suggested comments through your own experiences and feelings and come up with something you feel comfortable saying.

But as for you, continue in what you have learned and have become convinced of, because you know those from whom you learned it.
—2 Timothy 3:14

Today we're going to be talking about convictions. So, how many of you have been found guilty of a crime in a court of law? Oh, wait. Wrong kind of convictions. The convictions we're going to be talking about are the things we're convinced about, the beliefs we hold dear. Obviously it's not a new topic. After all, people have been talking about their convictions for thousands of years.

Read 2 Timothy 3:14 and continue.

Paul was telling his young friend Timothy to continue in what he had learned and what he had become convinced of.

Would you be willing to suffer for what you believe in? Would you be willing to change your life because of it? Would you be willing to give your life for a conviction? These are serious and important questions—questions that affect our everyday decisions and the way we live our lives.

Before you can know what you would be willing to do because of your convictions, you have to know what is it that you're convinced about. I'm not talking about being slightly convinced; I'm talking about being totally convinced. Things that you don't even question in your mind.

This would be the time for us to share some of our most strongly held convictions. Name it, explain how you came to believe the way you do, and tell how your conviction has affected your life. Be specific about what you believe. If it's appropriate and if you can, support your belief with Bible verses.

Convinced *20 min*

Next have the kids look at a few specific areas of their lives to see what kind of convictions they have in each one. Some of the categories are light and fun; others are serious. Let them know you think they can handle both kinds

Choose sentences from below that you think would work best for your group—or come up with some of your own. Encourage your kids to consider each question carefully before answering. After each person responds, allow the rest of the group to ask questions about the answer.

- **One thing I'm convinced about food is—**
- **One thing I'm convinced about the opposite sex is—**
- **One thing I'm convinced about money is—**
- **One thing I'm convinced about church is—**
- **One thing I'm convinced about the people in this group is—**
- **One thing I'm convinced about Jesus Christ is—**
- **One thing I'm convinced about myself is—**
- **One thing I'm convinced about marriage is—**
- **One thing I'm convinced about my most interesting class is—**
- **One thing I'm convinced about my best teacher is—**

trade secret

Pay close attention to your group members' responses. Take notes if that helps you, but do it discreetly. Your kids' answers may reveal some things about them you didn't know before, things that you might be able to use to enhance future conversations with them.

Did you hear that? *10 min*

Most of the exercises in today's session call for your kids to share. For a change of pace, wrap up your meeting with an activity that tests their listening skills. Explain it this way—

I'm going to start two sentences for you to finish. The first one calls for you to make a statement about the person on your right based on what you learned about that person in this meeting. The second one calls for you to make a statement about the person on your left, also based on what you learned about that person in this meeting.

Read the first statement below and then have the kids complete the sentence—one at a time—based on what they believe about the person to their right.

- **One thing I'm convinced about** [the person's name] **is—**

Do the same thing with the second statement about the person to the left.

- **After getting to know** [the person's name]**, I think that** [he or she] **is convinced that—**

PICTURE PAGE

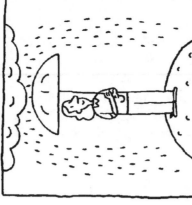

1.

2.

3.

PICTURE PAGE

1.

2.

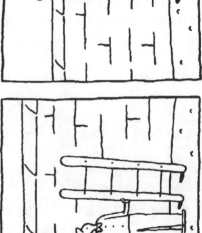

3.

picture THIS

The purpose of this meeting is to help your group members identify their goals in life.

In the beginning 5 min

Give your group members five minutes at the beginning of your meeting to catch up with each other's lives. Kids may talk in pairs, in trios, or as a large group, whatever they prefer. You might encourage them to seek out people they normally don't talk to, but beyond that don't interfere in this time of unstructured socializing. After five minutes or so, introduce the lesson this way—

For this meeting you'll need...

- Bibles

You guys are pretty good at communicating with words. But how good are you at communicating with pictures? We're going to find out today. Along the way, we'll also probably find out a little more about each other.

The future, as I picture it 15 min

Introduce this section by saying the first picture you want the kids to come up with is one about their futures. Tell them to imagine themselves exactly 10 years from right now. Give them a minute to get their pictures in focus. Then have them answer some questions about the picture they see. Use questions from the following list, depending on what you think will work with your group. For even better results, throw in a couple of your own future-related questions.

- **What part of the country or the world are you living in 10 years from now?**
- **Who is living with you?**
- **Are you married? If so, what does your spouse look like?**
- **Do you have any kids? If so, what do they look like? What are their names?**
- **What's your house like? How is it decorated?**
- **What do you do for a living? What kind of money do you make?**
- **What do you do for fun? What kind of hobbies are you into?**
- **In what ways are you different from the person you are today?**

Breaking tradition, you should probably encourage several volunteers to share their pictures with the group before you share yours, since it's likely that your picture will be quite different from your group members'.

After each person shares, allow the rest of the group to ask questions if you want to. If a person isn't specific enough in describing her picture, ask some clarifying questions. Be sure to give a word of encouragement or validation to each person who shares.

Snapshots from the mind's eye *15 min*

Let the kids know you think they have some pretty cool futures in mind. Then say something like—

I'd like to be around 10 years from now to see how accurate your pictures turn out to be. While we're on a roll with all of this mental picture stuff, let's keep going with some new topics. I'll give you a category, and you picture the details in your mind. Be as specific as possible with your images. When you've got the picture clear in your mind, describe it to the rest of us.

Encourage your group members to share their pictures for several of the following categories. If you think any of them won't work with your group, substitute your own ideas.

- **Picture your future spouse.**
- **Picture a happy family.**
- **Picture a very good friendship.**
- **Picture total disappointment.**
- **Picture a disaster.**
- **Picture God.**
- **Picture some kind of wipe-out.**
- **Picture a successful person.**
- **Picture a romantic date.**

After each person shares, let the rest of the group ask questions if they like. If necessary, you also should ask some questions to help your volunteers explain their pictures.

The encounter *15 min*

Tell the kids you've got one last picture for them to think of. Have them picture as clearly as they can what it would be like if Jesus were to make an appointment with them for tomorrow afternoon. Set up the situation like this—

> Let's say Jesus lets you know he wants to meet with you tomorrow afternoon at 2:00. You're going to be alone with Jesus for one hour. Listen quietly while I read the following description. Use your imagination to picture the situation as clearly as you can.
>
> As soon as you get up in the morning, you remember your meeting. You get dressed. You go to school. What are your feelings as the hours go by and you start to anticipate the meeting? You go to the building where you're supposed to meet. It's very quiet. You know your meeting is in the first room on the right. You go in. There he is. What's he doing? What's he wearing? He greets you. What does he say? You look at him. He asks you to sit down. You talk for quite awhile. What do you talk about? When your time is up, you stand. Now what do you do? After the meeting, you go out to your car to think about what just happened.

Your group members will likely have very different ideas about what this imaginary encounter would be like. Ask them to share their pictures one at a time as you ask questions like these—

- What are you thinking or worrying about while you're waiting for meeting time?
- What's Jesus doing when you first see him?
- What does he look like? What's he wearing?
- What does he say when he meets you?
- What do you talk about?
- What do you do at the end of the meeting?
- How will your life change as a result of the meeting?

Says you *5 min*

Remind the group that the people in New Testament times didn't have to picture what it would be like to talk to Jesus—they could actually do it! For example, John 9 tells about a man who was born blind. Recount for the group how—on what had to have been the best day of his life—this man met Jesus. Continue with comments something like these—

Now you can probably guess what happened when Jesus encountered this guy who couldn't see. That's right, Jesus gave him back his sight. When the people of Jerusalem saw that the man had been healed, they wanted to know what had happened. The man was more than happy to tell them about Jesus. The religious leaders who wanted to get rid of Jesus weren't real happy to hear the ex-blind man's story, so they threw him out of the synagogue.

Let's pick up the story in verse 35 to see how the man responded to Jesus.

Read John 9:35-38.

All right, that's how one man responded to Jesus. Now what about you? What's your response to Jesus? Is he real in your life? I've asked myself that same question. I'd like you to ask yourself: is Jesus real in your life? If not, what can you do to make him real?

Jesus heard that they had thrown him out, and when he found him, he said, "Do you believe in the Son of Man?"

"Who is he, sir?" the man asked. "Tell me so that I may believe in him."

Jesus said, "You have now seen him; in fact, he is the one speaking with you."

Then the man said, "Lord, I believe," and he worshiped him.

—John 9:35-38

Did you hear that? *5 min*

Wrap up the meeting with a quick listening exercise. Tell the kids you would like each one to name one thing you heard someone say during this meeting that was particularly interesting or memorable. Start the exercise yourself, then encourage someone else to follow your example by commenting on another memorable remark. Continue until everyone in the group has shared.

best FRIENDS

The purpose of this meeting is to help your group members understand the importance of Christian friendship.

In the beginning *15 min*

Kick off your meeting with a mini-survey of your group members. Put this question to them—

What are the three most important things in your life?

Write your kids' answers on the board. Pay particular attention to the ones who list friends among their top three priorities.

Throw out one or more of the following questions for discussion.

- **Why are friends so important?**
- **What do your friends add to your life?**
- **What's the best kind of friend to have?**

Hand out the blank paper and the pencils. Explain the next activity something like this—

Let's spend a few minutes thinking about friendships—the way the people in your life relate to you and each other. On your index card I want you to draw circles to represent you and your friends, and the way your relationships work.

Each circle will represent one friend. Write the person's name or initials in the circle. Before you do that, though, position the circles in a

For this meeting you'll need...

- Whiteboard and markers
- Blank paper
- Pencils
- Bibles

trade secret

Instead of a whiteboard you can use a chalkboard, butcher paper taped to the wall, overhead, or any other suitable option. The main idea is to be able to jot down ideas so everyone can see them.

Don't overlook the fact that this could be a potentially upsetting exercise for some of your kids. If one of your group members assumed that she was friends with another but doesn't see her name on the other person's diagram, she might be hurt. That's why it's important that you not put any pressure on your kids to share their diagrams if they don't want to.

way that shows how you and your friends relate to each other. For example, if your friends revolve around you, put yourself in the middle with your closest friends near you. If you have a best friend, draw that person's circle closest to you. If you have two separate groups of friends, show that on your card. Do your best to make your diagram as realistic as possible.

After a few minutes, ask volunteers to display and explain their diagrams.

Says you *10 min*

Ask the kids a question like this—

If you had to compare a good friend to something, what would it be? For example, maybe you think of a friend as a psychiatrist, someone you can tell your deepest secrets to. Or maybe you'd compare a good friend to a faithful dog, someone who's there when you need him and who likes you despite your faults. Tell us how you picture a good friend.

After several of your group members have shared their comparisons, throw out one of your own.

What would you say if I compared a good friend to a stretcher carrier—you know, a person like a paramedic or firefighter who carries injured people on stretchers? Think about it. A stretcher carrier helps people when they're most vulnerable. She supports them when they need it most.

Encourage at least a couple of your kids to share their reactions to your analogy. When they're finished, reveal where the comparison comes from. Read Mark 2:1-12. Then discuss the passage using one or more of the following questions.

A few days later, when Jesus again entered Capernaum, the people heard that he had come home. So many gathered that there was no room left, not even outside the door, and he preached the word to them. Some men came, bringing to him a paralytic, carried by four of them. Since they could not get him to Jesus because of the crowd, they made an opening in the roof above Jesus and, after digging through it, lowered the mat the paralyzed man was lying on. When Jesus saw their faith, he said to the paralytic, "Son, your sins are forgiven."

Now some teachers of the law were sitting there, thinking to themselves, "Why does this fellow talk like that? He's blaspheming! Who can forgive sins but God alone?"

Immediately Jesus knew in his spirit that this was what they were thinking in their hearts, and he said to them, "Why are you thinking these things? Which is easier: to say to the paralytic, 'Your sins are forgiven,' or to say, 'Get up, take your mat and walk'? But that you may know that the Son of Man has authority on earth to forgive sins. . . ." He said to the paralytic, "I tell you, get up, take your mat and go home." He got up, took his mat and walked out in full view of them all. This amazed everyone and they praised God, saying, "We have never seen anything like this!"

—Mark 2:1-12

- On a scale of one to 10, with one being a terrible friend and 10 being the best friend in the world, how would you rate the stretcher carriers in this story?
- What do you think the four stretcher carriers were like as people? What characteristics did they have that made them good friends?
- Why do you suppose the four men were so willing to help their friend?
- What do you suppose happened to the men's friendship after the five of them returned home?
- What's the most extreme thing a friend has done for you?
- What's the most extreme thing you've ever done for a friend?

84

Suggest to your kids that stretcher-carrying is a continuous process in friendship. If right now you're not on a stretcher yourself, being carried and supported by friends, you should be willing and available to carry a stretcher for someone else.

Finish the— 20 *min*

Tell the kids that whether they're being carried or doing the carrying themselves, they must admit that good friends—like those who carried the crippled man—are important in life. Now have the group focus more on this idea of true friendship. Read the beginning of some sentences and let the kids finish them, expressing their honest feelings about friendship.

Depending on how well you think they'll work with your group, use any or all of the following sentences to prompt discussion and opinion-sharing among your kids.

- **One thing to remember about helping a friend in need is—**
- **The last time a friend really came through for me was—**
- **The last time a friend really dropped the ball when I needed my friend was—**
- **One thing that bothers me about carrying someone else's stretcher is—**
- **One thing about God's friendship that encourages me is—**

Group in focus 15 *min*

Wrap up your session with a few more sentence starters, this time focusing on your group members' relationships with each other.

- **One thing I need from my friends in this group is—**
- **One thing I need from [the name of a person in your group] is—**
- **One way this group encourages and helps me is—**
- **One way I want to help carry a stretcher for someone else is—**

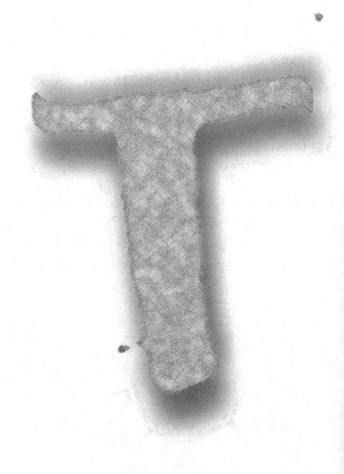

family BUSINESS

The purpose of this meeting is to help your group members learn how to improve their family relationships.

Finish the— *20 min*

Today we're going to be talking about family—mothers, fathers, sisters, brothers, and anyone else who makes up your family. Regardless of how you feel about your family these days, I hope you'll be honest with us. You can count on the fact that what is said in this room stays in this room. So feel free to open up with us. In fact, you can start right now by finishing the following sentences.

> **For this meeting you'll need...**
> • Bibles

Encourage most, if not all, of your kids to share their responses with the group. Set a good example for them by completing each sentence first yourself.

Use any or all of the following sentence starters, depending on how well you think they'll work with your group. Feel free to add or substitute your own, as necessary.

- One of the happiest times I've ever spent with my family is—
- One of the saddest times I've ever spent with my family is—
- One of the most boring times I've ever spent with my family is—
- If you really want to see my family get tense, all you have to do is—
- The family vacation I remember best is—
- The best thing about my family is—
- The worst thing about my family is—

trade secret
Be on the lookout for teachable moments and special needs each week. There may be occasions when kids come to your meeting with urgent concerns or pressing issues on their minds. Remember, their needs are more important than this curriculum. Put the lesson on the back burner while you address your kids' issues as a group, if you need to. Tell the kids that today's topic may be popular with some of them and unpopular with others.

This time it's personal *15 min*

Encourage the group with how well they did on the first round of completing sentences. Now they're ready for Round Two. Warn the kids the sentences are going to get a little more personal.

Again, choose the sentence starters that will work best for your group and ignore the rest.

- **My room looks like—**
- **Of the Fourth of July, my mom's birthday, and Easter, the holiday I enjoy the most is—**
- **The person in my family who I'm closest to is—**
- **The TV family most like mine is—**
- **The topic that causes the most arguments in my family is—**
- **My family's attitude toward God is—**
- **If I could change one thing in my family, I'd change—**
- **One thing I could do to make my family life better is—**

trade secret
You'll be setting the pace for your group members in this activity. The more openness, honesty, and vulnerability you show in responding to these statements, the more likely your kids will follow suit. Remind your group members they have the option to pass if they're not comfortable with responding to a statement.

Says you *10 min*

Remind the kids that they may not know it, but the Bible has a lot to say about families. Use comments along these lines—

> If we had time, I could read you dozens of family-related verses. But I'll give you a break this time and read only two of them—one from the Old Testament and one from the New Testament. Let's start with the Old Testament.

Read Exodus 20:12. Use one or more of the following questions to guide your discussion of the verse.

- **What does it mean to honor your father and your mother?**
- **What are some things that make it hard to honor your parents?**
- **What steps can you take to honor your parents this week?**

Honor your father and your mother, so that you may live long in the land the Lord your God is giving you.
—Exodus 20:12

Read 1 Timothy 4:12. Use any or all of these questions to lead your group members in discussing the verse.

- **What does it mean to set an example in your speech, life, love, faith, and purity?**
- **What would happen if you tried to set these examples around your family?**
- **What might make it hard for you to set an example for your family in these areas?**
- **What can you do this week to set an example for your family in one or more of these areas?**

Don't let anyone look down on you because you are young, but set an example for the believers in speech, in life, in love, in faith and in purity.
—1 Timothy 4:12

Did you hear that? *15 min*

As you wrap up the session, try a listening activity with your kids. Choose one person from the group to focus on at a time. You and your group members should then take turns recalling information you learned about the person's family or memorable things the person said during the meeting. Try to have at least three people in the group contribute a recollection for each person.

As usual, you'll probably need to take the lead in this exercise. Choose one person from the group and say something perhaps a bit lighthearted like this—

Nadia, one thing I learned about your family today is that I never want to take a vacation to Mexico with your dad—especially if he drinks the water there.

After you start the ball rolling, encourage your group members to follow suit, commenting on what they learned about the person's family. After three (or more) of your kids have shared, choose another person in the group to focus on. Continue until everyone has had her turn in the spotlight.

trade secret
After the meeting, make it a point to seek out your group members individually to thank them for coming and let them know how glad you are that they're part of your group.

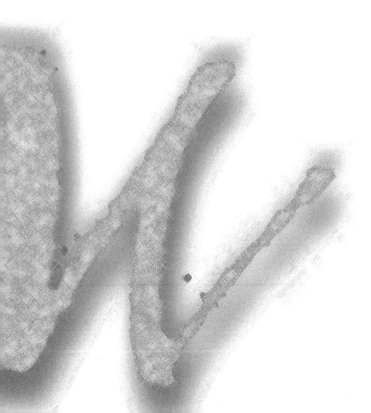

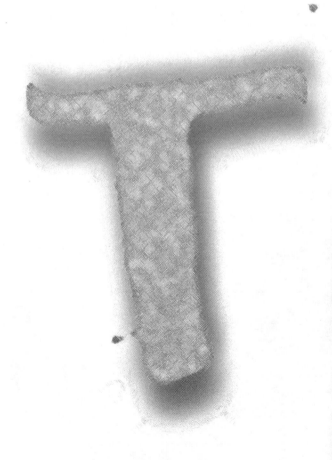

ch-ch-ch- CHANGES

The purpose of this meeting is to help your group members consider the past, present, and future changes in their lives.

In the beginning *10 min*

Take a few minutes at the beginning of your meeting to get filled in on the things that are going on in your kids' lives. Ask each group member to share one thing that happened to her during the past week. It could be something that occurred at home, at school, at work, with friends, or when he was alone. After sharing your personal-life update first, listen intently to the things your kids share. Make a note—mental or written—of follow-up questions you'd like to ask specific group members after the meeting.

> **For this meeting you'll need...**
>
> • Bibles

Off-site fellowship *25 min*

Start out by saying something like—

> **As you've probably come to realize, life is full of changes. Some are good; others are difficult.**

Assign each person in the group a partner. If you have an odd number of group members, join the exercise yourself to even things out. Let the kids know you want each pair to talk about changes they've experienced by saying something like—

> **You and your partner will have 15 minutes to talk about ways you've changed since grade school, about half the time for each of you. While**

you share, your partner should ask questions to try to understand the ways you're now different. When I give you the signal, let's regroup here. Then we'll share what we learn.

Let them scatter to the far corners of the room, move to another room, or perhaps venture outside, depending on your meeting area.

After you reassemble the group, ask each student to give a brief report of what he learned about the changes in his partner's life. If you need to, ask a few questions of your own to get a better understanding of your group members' personal evolution.

still changin'  5 min

Acknowledge how different the group members were in grade school and how much everyone has changed. And is *still* changing.

Of course, those changes haven't stopped. All of us in this room are still changing. Change is a continuous process. I'll give you some examples.

Share with your group members a couple of ways you're currently experiencing change. For example, if you're not married, you may be thinking about what it would be like to settle down. Or, if you're married, you may be thinking about what it would be like to have kids. If you want your kids to share personal information with you, you should be prepared to share appropriate personal information with them.

After you've finished revealing some of your current areas of change, ask for volunteers to share one way they are experiencing change. Encourage, but don't force, most of your kids to respond.

future changes 10 min

Past, present…okay, now what about the future? Tell the kids that you realize most them probably have some good ideas as to how they might change in the future—or at least how they'd *like* to change in the future.

As you think about the kind of person you'd like to become, name some specific ways in which you'd like to change. Maybe you'd like to do something about your education, your home, your faith, your family, your friends, whatever. Think seriously about your future changes for a minute.

After your kids have given some thought to the issue, ask several of them to share the changes they see or hope for in their future. You don't have to go first this time, but you should be prepared to share at some point during the discussion.

Says you *10 min*

The ideas in this section are provided to give you a starting place to build on. Fill them in (or substitute them) with details from your own life to make your talk as personal as possible.

We all have changed and will continue to change. That's a fact of life. Every day brings new experiences that affect and change us. It's part of being a human being. God, on the other hand, is not like that. God doesn't change. He's the same yesterday, today, and tomorrow. That's important for me to keep in mind. I can count on my heavenly Father. I don't have to worry about him suddenly changing his mind about something or gradually changing the way he feels about me. God will never change.

The Book of James in the New Testament says that all good gifts in life come from God and that the Giver does not change.

Read James 1:17.

Before the meeting, spend some time thinking about this verse and why it's important to you. At this point in the meeting, share with your kids what you come up with. Then get their opinions on the subject, using the questions and comments like these—

Which part of God's unchanging nature are you especially thankful for? With God, there are a lot of characteristics to choose from. Don't worry about saying the wrong thing, because there aren't right or wrong answers. For example, God's presence might be the characteristic you're most thankful for. It may be important for you to know that God is always with you. Or you may be thankful for God's forgiveness, how he's always willing to take you back when you turn from the things you do wrong. Or maybe you're thankful that God is always waiting for you in heaven. Whatever you're thankful for, tell us about it.

Encourage most, if not all, of your group members to share the unchangeable characteristics of God that are most important to them.

You've changed *10 min*

Tell the kids that whether they realize it or not, everyone has changed since the group began getting together.

It's been interesting for me to see both our changes as individuals and the changes in our group. I would like each of us to make one observation about a change we've seen in another person in the group. I'll give you a minute or two to think, then I'll begin.

trade secret

It's important that you present yourself as an equal participant during most of your small group meeting time. However, this is a special time for you—as leader, not as participant—to share some brief, significant point that is close to your heart. Ideally the information you share should relate to the things your group has just talked about and should have practical application in your kids' lives. Remember, young people are usually more interested in learning from life's experiences than from curriculum.

Every good and perfect gift is from above, coming down from the Father of the heavenly lights, who does not change like shifting shadows.

—James 1:17

Share a change you've noticed in one of your group members. Then ask that person to share a change he's noticed in someone else. Continue until everyone has had an opportunity to share.

Wrap up the session by listing some ways your whole group has changed since the first meeting. This will be a great chance for you to affirm the increased growth, honesty, and openness you've seen in your group members.

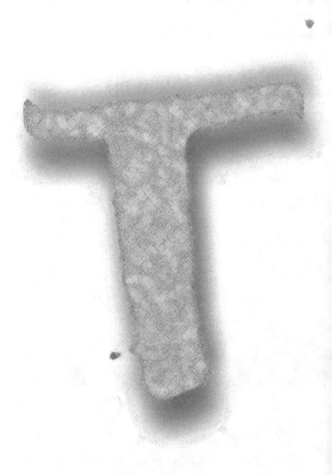

all you need is LOVE

The purpose of this meeting is to help your group members consider how they give and receive love with their parents, peers, and God.

In the beginning *10 min*

Start out by informing the group members that for this meeting you'll be breaking tradition. Instead of having everyone in the group telling something that happened in the past week, each kid will share something that happened to *someone else* in the group. After each person shares what she knows, give the group member in question a chance to react to or dispute the update. Keep the mood light during this exercise. Have fun!

> **For this meeting you'll need...**
> - Paper
> - Pencils
> - Bibles

What's love? *20 min*

Quickly divide the group into two or three teams. Give each team a piece of paper, a pencil, and two minutes to list as many songs as the members can think of that mention or deal with love in the lyrics. When time is up, have each team quickly read its list. Give a round of applause (or a small prize, if you're feeling generous) to the team that comes up with the most titles. Mention a few of the songs listed. Then say something like—

> **All right, we hear songs about love every day. We see people fall in love in the movies and on TV all of the time. So we should know quite a bit about the subject, right? So tell me—what is love?**

If and when your kids are finally able to reach a consensus in defining love, give them another thing to think about. What's the best way to show love to another person? Let your group members wrestle with their responses for a minute or two. Eventually they may come to the conclusion that everyone shows love differently, that there is no best way to show love. Then ask something like—

What are some of the best ways to show love to you? What are some of the worst ways?

These questions call not only for some soul searching on the part of your group members, but also some vulnerability in sharing their responses with the rest of the group. Help your kids see that what feels like love to one person may not feel like love to another person.

If you find that your group members are reluctant to answer, try another approach. Read a list of actions and have your group members hoot and holler—or whatever works for your group—each time they think an action is an expression of love.

Use the items below that will work best with your group members or add your own ideas.

- **Your parents set a curfew for you.**
- **Your mom makes you study and get your homework done every night.**
- **Your dad gives you a new car.**
- **Your parents ask you questions about what's going on in your life.**
- **Your grandfather hugs you.**
- **Your grandmother says, "I love you."**
- **The person you're dating holds your hand.**
- **The person you're dating calls you every night and talks for at least an hour.**
- **The person you're dating wants you all to herself and doesn't want you to talk with anyone else.**
- **The person you're dating asks to marry you.**

After you've gone through the list, personalize your discussion a little more by thinking about questions like these—

- **Describe two different ways that your parents give love to you.**
- **Describe two different ways that you try to give love to your parents.**
- **How well do your parents receive the love that you try to give?**
- **How do you and your friends express love or care for each other?**

Encourage your group members to share openly and honestly in response to these questions—it may make a significant difference in your group dynamics.

Love scenes *15 min*

The next exercise calls for creativity so affirm your kids for their imaginations. One at a time, have group members describe a scene that illustrates when, where, and how they feel the most loved as a person. Give some examples.

You may describe walking hand in hand with your girlfriend on a beach at sunset. You may be sitting up late at night with your sister or brother, talking about ideas that are important to you. You may describe opening an unbelievable gift on Christmas morning. Just make sure that the scene you describe comes straight from your heart.

Encourage your group members to listen intently to each other's descriptions. What better way to show you care about people than by showing keen interest in their thoughts and experiences?

Of course, as the fearless leader of the group, you should be the first one to share your love scene.

The greatest love of all *20 min*

As the meeting begins to draw to a close, you can remind the group that as far as you're concerned, no one can talk about true love without talking about God, the one who gave us the ability to love. Put it into words like these—

God loves every person in this room more than we could ever imagine. Time and time again he has shown his love for us in many different ways. First of all, he created us and the world we live in. Then he gave us his son, Jesus, to die for us. He forgives us when we disobey him. He's prepared an incredible future home for us. He's always available to help us when we need him. He gave us the Bible to help us live.

Read John 3:16.

Wrap up the session by asking your group members to answer a few more questions about love—specifically, God's love for your group members and their love for each other.

- **Have you ever felt especially loved by God? What it was like? What was the situation? How did his love feel?**

- **How have we, as a small group, shown each other love and concern? How can we continue to show love for each other in the future?**

For God so loved the world that he gave his one and only Son, that whoever believes in him shall not perish but have eternal life.
—John 3:16

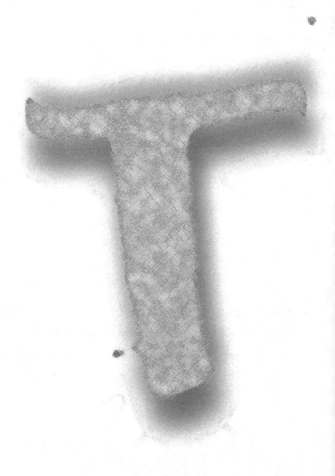

agree to DISAGREE

The purpose of this meeting is to help your group members learn to maintain friendships with people who disagree with them on important issues.

In the beginning *15 min*

Single out an athlete in your group and ask her this question—

What's the most important thing to do before a game, a practice, or a workout?

For this meeting you'll need...

- Index cards prepared according to the instructions on page 101

The answer you're looking for is stretch or warm up. Coaches and trainers will say that if you don't stretch before you start working out, you risk injuring yourself. Let them know you're going to take their advice for this meeting. Say something like—

We've got a lot of things to talk about as a group today. I don't want you spraining a vocal cord or pulling a tongue muscle, so we're going to do some small warm-up discussions to begin with. I'll divide you into pairs and give you a topic to discuss. Each person in the pair will have about a minute to talk. When time is up, I'll say "Switch," you'll find another partner, and I'll give you another topic.

As much as possible, try to pair up kids who don't usually spend a lot of time together. Encourage the pairs to spread out to the far corners of the room. Keep an eye on the clock, calling out "Switch" and a new topic, every two minutes or so. The following list will get you started. Feel free to add others that will go over well with your kids.

- **Tell your partner about something you achieved this week.**
- **Tell your partner about how you wasted some time this week.**
- **Tell your partner about something that really frustrated you this week.**
- **Tell your partner about something you and one of your good friends did this week.**
- **Tell your partner about a good time you had this week.**

After your kids have switched partners a few times, bring the group back together. Point to one person in the circle and ask—

What did you learn about [the person's name] **today?**

The group members who had that person as a partner can share what they discovered. Continue until everyone in the group has been profiled.

A little friendly controversy 5 min

Tell the group that after you read a sentence, they should stand up if they believe what you've said is true. If they don't believe it's true, they should stay seated.

- **True friends usually agree with each other about most things.**
- **It's okay to be friends with people who disagree with you about major issues in life.**
- **It's wrong for Christians to be friends with non-Christians.**
- **It's impossible to truly respect someone who doesn't share your deepest beliefs.**

Encourage your group members to respond honestly to these questions, even if they happen to be part of the minority opinion. After the questions, continue along these lines—

Believe it or not, disagreement and even controversy between friends can be good—if it's handled well. That's what we're going to be talking about today—how to maintain friendships with people we disagree with.

Some people have a tough time being friends with anyone who strongly disagrees with them. That's too bad. Those people are missing out on some interesting learning opportunities and fulfilling friendships.

It's possible to respect and appreciate people who hold different views than we do—even when it comes to the most controversial subjects. It's simply a matter of learning to agree to disagree and not allowing issues to destroy relationships.

choosing your battles *10 min*

Before the session you'll need to prepare an index card for each group member. On each card write a list of controversial topics. Below you'll find some ideas to get you started. Feel free to add your own, based on what you think will push your group members' buttons.

- **Is homosexuality wrong?**
- **Is sex before marriage harmful?**
- **Is every word of the Bible true?**
- **Is abortion murder?**
- **Is it wrong to want to own really nice things?**
- **Are most churchgoers hypocrites?**
- **Is it true that cheaters never win?**
- **Is there anything wrong with pornography?**
- **Should Christians fight in a war?**

Hand out the cards and ask your group members to choose the topic they would most like to discuss. One at a time, have your kids share their selections. Keep a tally to see which two or three topics are most interesting to your group. Select one of them to begin your discussion time.

I believe— *30 min*

Continue the meeting by introducing the subject you chose with words something like—

The first controversial topic we're going to talk about is _____. Obviously the first thing we need to do in our discussion is share our feelings on the topic. Tell us how you feel about the issue, how strong your convictions are, and why you feel the way you do. Make sure, though, that you begin each statement with "I"—as in "I think," "I believe," "I know," or "I feel strongly." Remember, all you're sharing is your opinion. Make sure you keep your comments focused on the topic, not on other people in the group.

To begin the discussion call on someone who appears ready to talk. After everyone has shared, encourage those who feel most strongly about the issue to express more of their beliefs and reasoning.

Allow the discussion to build for several minutes or until you notice that no new ideas are surfacing. Don't be afraid to share your own beliefs, though you may want to wait until everyone else has shared so that you don't unwittingly influence someone else's opinion.

Continue the process with the favorite two or three topics your kids selected. Ideally you'll generate some heated (though controlled) discussion among your group members. Don't discourage any arguments—unless, of course, they don't meet the guidelines you gave at the beginning.

After you've exhausted your group's most popular controversial topics, it's time to introduce the idea of friendship in the midst of controversy.

We mentioned earlier that friendship and disagreement can go together. Now let's put our money where our mouths are. I want each of you to think of someone in the group that you disagree with. First, I want you to say something positive and sincere to that person. Second, I want you to explain to the person what it is you disagree with. Here are some examples.

- **"Willie, I really enjoy having you in our small group, but I don't agree with you when you say that it doesn't really matter what a person believes about God."**
- **"Magdalena, I consider you to be a good friend, but I completely disagree with what you said about sex before marriage."**
- **"Chris, you're a really smart guy, but I have to disagree with your opinions on abortion."**

Says you *5 min*

Incorporate the skills your group members just practiced into your session-closing time. Use comments like the following to introduce the exercise.

For weeks now I've been sharing little bits and pieces about my values and beliefs. You know that I'm a Christian and that I believe God communicates to us through the Bible and that each of us must make a decision about whether we'll live our lives for Jesus. You know many other things about me.

Mention some other things you've shared about yourself, such as the fact that you love your wife, the fact that you enjoy your children, the fact that you sometimes lose your temper in traffic, and so on.

From the information you give them, your group members should try to come up with the same kind of two-part statements they worked on earlier. In other words, your kids will be practicing their disagreeing-with-friends skills on you. First, they should say something positive about you; then they should explain what it is they disagree with.

the PROS & CONS of INTIMACY

The purpose of this meeting is to help your group members understand why intimacy is important in relationships.

In the beginning *15 min*

Start the meeting by saying something like this—

Today we're going to be talking about intimacy—not the husband-and-wife physical kind of intimacy, but emotional intimacy.

But before we get too deeply involved in that topic, I want to know what's happened in your life since the last time I saw you. I'm going to read a few sentence starters, and I want you to fill in the blanks with details from your life.

For this meeting you'll need...

- An egg
- Bibles

Pick some of the following sentence starters. Encourage most of your group members to finish the thoughts.

- I had a really good time this week when—
- I got into trouble this week when—
- I was stressed out this week when—
- I laughed really hard this week when—
- I learned something this week when—
- I had a great talk this week with _____ about—

An intimate encounter 5 *min*

So that your group members are all on the same page, make sure they all know what you're talking about when you mention intimacy. Take a minute or two to have several volunteers offer their definitions of the word. If no one nails the concept, suggest that intimacy means being very personal, close, or familiar.

Intimate friendships are something that most people want to develop. However, those kinds of friendship require skill and vulnerability. You take a risk every time you try to be intimate with another person. You risk being laughed at, rejected, or ignored.

Of course, the rewards of an intimate friendship are worth the risk. It makes me feel good to share my deepest thoughts, feelings, and questions with a friend. These are things that I don't share with many people, so when I find someone I can trust with that information it's special to me.

You'll need an egg for the next activity. Show it to your group members while you continue talking.

People are like eggs. At first touch an egg seems hard. But you and I know that on the inside of the hard outer shell is a soft inner part. In many ways I'm like an egg. I protect my inner feelings with an outer shell. But that shell is only a protective device. Aside from that, it's useless. The valuable part of an egg—and me—is inside the shell. Intimacy is letting people inside my shell. It involves sharing some of the important stuff inside me with a good friend.

Handling eggs and people is a delicate business. They're easily destroyed. When we experience intimacy with people, we must be very careful and respectful.

Inside the shell 30 *min*

Use the egg as a discussion starter among your group members. Pass it around the circle. When a person receives the egg, he gets to complete two sentences—

- **Just as an egg has a shell, I have a shell of protection. The way I build my shell of protection is—**
- **When the egg's shell is broken, you can see what's inside. One fear I have in cracking my shell and letting people see what's inside me is—**

After the first person is finished, pass the egg until everyone has had a turn with the two sentences. When the egg has made its first round, continue the pass-and-share process with sentence starters that call for more personal reflections. Use any or all of the following ideas, depending on what you think will work best for each group member. You may want to remind your kids they don't have to answer any question they're uncomfortable with.

- **One thing that makes me hurt inside is—**
- **One thing that scares me is—**
- **One thing I keep hidden inside is—**
- **The way I really feel about myself inside is—**
- **When I think about my family, I feel—**
- **When I think about faith in Jesus, I feel—**
- **The way I feel about this sharing exercise is—**

Says you *15 min*

For maximum dramatic effect (and to get more mileage out of this session's object lesson), hold the egg up while you talk, saying like—

As we said, handling eggs is a delicate business. So is caring about people. Fortunately for us, God is in the business of caring for people. He knows all about us and loves us. You might even say he cherishes us. He knows both our outside shells and our inner thoughts and feelings.

In Luke 15, Jesus tells a great story about a father and son. Listen closely as I read it. Even though some of you may know the story, you might pick up some new details. Pay special attention to the people's feelings in the story.

Read Luke 15:11-32.

This is a sad story with a happy ending. It's interesting that the father didn't leave his house to go after his son or hire a bounty hunter to bring him home. He just waited. He waited for his son to come to his senses and change inside. He waited for him to want to come home.

God is that Father for us. He's waiting for you and me to want to make changes in our lives. But he's waiting patiently. He never forces his will on us. He waits for us to look for it.

Pass the egg around your circle one more time. Ask each group member to complete this statement—

I think God is waiting for me to—

Jesus continued: "There was a man who had two sons. The younger one said to his father, 'Father, give me my share of the estate.' So he divided his property between them.

"Not long after that, the younger son got together all he had, set off for a distant country and there squandered his wealth in wild living. After he had spent everything, there was a severe famine in that whole country, and he began to be in need. So he went and hired himself out to a citizen of that country, who sent him to his fields to feed pigs. He longed to fill his stomach with the pods that the pigs were eating, but no one gave him anything.

"When he came to his senses, he said, 'How many of my father's hired men have food to spare, and here I am starving to death! I will set out and go back to my father and say to him: Father, I have sinned against heaven and against you. I am no longer worthy to be called your son; make me like one of your hired men.' So he got up and went to his father.

"But while he was still a long way off, his father saw him and was filled with compassion for him; he ran to his son, threw his arms around him and kissed him.

"The son said to him, 'Father, I have sinned against heaven and against you. I am no longer worthy to be called your son.'

"But the father said to his servants, 'Quick! Bring the best robe and put it on him. Put a ring on his finger and sandals on his feet. Bring the fattened calf and kill it. Let's have a feast and celebrate. For this son of mine was dead and is alive again; he was lost and is found.' So they began to celebrate.

"Meanwhile, the older son was in the field. When he came near the house, he heard music and dancing. So he called one of the servants and asked him what was going on. 'Your brother has come,' he replied, 'and your father has killed the fattened calf because he has him back safe and sound.'

"The older brother became angry and refused to go in. So his father went out and pleaded with him. But he answered his father, 'Look! All these years I've been slaving for you and never disobeyed your orders. Yet you never gave me even a young goat so I could celebrate with my friends. But when this son of yours who has squandered your property with prostitutes comes home, you kill the fattened calf for him!'

"'My son,' the father said, 'you are always with me, and everything I have is yours. But we had to celebrate and be glad, because this brother of yours was dead and is alive again; he was lost and is found.' "

—Luke 15:11-32

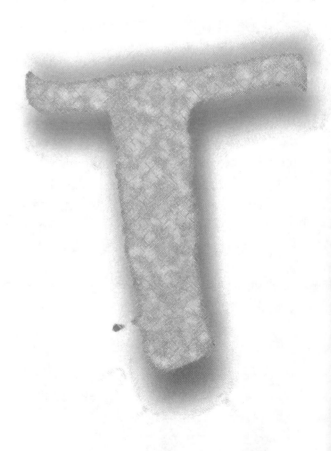

GUTS & GLORY

The purpose of this meeting is to help your group members evaluate their own courage.

Par-ty! Par-ty! Par-ty! *10 min*

Create a party atmosphere for the first 10 minutes of your meeting. Rather than making your group members sit in a circle right away, let them wander around the room, mingling and greeting each other. Bring in some snacks for them to munch on.

In the midst of the festivities, ask your kids to find a discussion partner. (If you have an odd number of kids, you'll need to pair up with a teen, too.) Give the pairs a topic to discuss for one minute. When you call "Switch," your kids change partners. Continue the activity until everyone has had four or five partners.

Use any or all of the following topics for your party conversations.

For this meeting you'll need...

- Whatever supplies and snacks you want to create a party atmosphere
- Copies of **Comfort Zone** (page 110)
- Bibles

- **Things that happened at school this week**
- **Family news**
- **Sports and hobby news**
- **Plans for the coming months**
- **TV shows and movies**
- **Things you want to buy**
- **How you would spend $10,000 in one day**
- **The best vacation you can think of**
- **The best party you've ever attended**

Talk across *10 min*

Tell the group members that you don't know how hard the partner-switching exercise was for them, but this next activity will be harder. Explain how it works something like this—

> **We're going to pull our chairs into a circle, and I'm going to assign you a partner who's sitting across the circle from you. Without moving, we're all going to try to talk to our partners at the same time. I'll warn you—it's going to get loud in here. You're going to have to focus on what your partner is saying. To begin I want you to talk about some of the most dangerous things you've ever done. You might talk about riding with a crazy driver, skiing a double diamond run, climbing a mountain, or even just being honest with your dad. Ready, go!**

After several minutes of chaos, restore some order to the group. Talk about the activity with your kids. Find out how much they were able to learn about their partner.

Finish the— *15 min*

Next announce that this meeting's topic is courage. Say something like—

> **Are any of you afraid of that topic? No? Well, that's a good start. Now let's see if you've got the guts to finish these sentences by sharing your true feelings.**

Demonstrate some of your own courage by finishing each sentence first yourself. Remember, the more open and honest you are, the more likely your kids will be open and honest, too.

Use some of these ideas—

- **If I had more courage I'd like to—**
- **One person who I think has a lot of courage is—**
- **One of the bravest things I've ever done is—**
- **If I had more courage in my relationship with a friend, I would—**
- **I do (or don't) consider myself courageous because—**

Comfort zone *15 min*

Before the session, you'll need to make copies of **Comfort Zone** on page 110. Hand out the copies to your group members. Give them a minute to look over the diagram. Use or adapt the following questions to lead your kids in discussing the illustration.

- **Why do you suppose comfort is shown as a pit?**
- **Describe how being comfortable in your life can become a trap to you.**
- **What does the arrow tell you about the relationship between comfort and courage?**
- **Why does it take courage to leave your comfort zone?**
- **Describe how a person might show courage in leaving his comfortable surroundings.**
- **How does courage lead to growth?**

Encourage your group members to offer their opinions. Once you've gotten your kids comfortable with answering courage-related questions, move the discussion into more personal territory. Some questions to guide your conversation—

- **Describe a comfortable rut that you're in right now.**
- **Describe a time in your life when you had the courage to be uncomfortable.**
- **Describe one step of courage and discomfort that you need to take soon.**

Says you *10 min*

Here's an analogy that you might want to share at this point.

Many things in life take courage—including living a life that's pleasing to Jesus. Sometimes I think of it like this—I'm walking behind Jesus up a foggy mountainside. He wants me to follow him and do the things that he does.

Sometimes I feel close to him and can see him clearly. That's when it's fun to follow him. Sometimes, though, the fog gets thick, and I can just barely see him in the distance ahead of me. That's when I get scared.

Sometimes on really bad days, I lose sight of him altogether for awhile. I know he's still ahead of me, but I can't see him. I wonder if he knows that I'm still following him. I wonder if I'm going in the right direction. I become afraid to take the next step. It takes a lot of courage to continue on, believing that I'll be safe.

Read Luke 14:27.

And anyone who does not carry his cross and follow me cannot be my disciple.
—Luke 14:27

Carrying a cross means doing something difficult or that I wouldn't normally do because I love Jesus. Following him takes courage.

Wrap up this session by asking volunteers to share things about the Christian faith that take courage. As a group, discuss ways in which Christians can build up their courage.

Comfort Zone

the opposite SEX

The purpose of this meeting is to encourage discussion, understanding, and appreciation between your male and female group members.

In the beginning *10 min*

Gather the group together and say something like—

Believe it or not, during this meeting we're going to try to figure out the opposite sex. Obviously we'll need all the time we can get to do that, so today when we share about our weeks, we're going to limit the description to three words or less.

For this meeting you'll need...

- Copies of the **Rate Your Week** (page 115)
- Blank index cards
- Pencils
- Bibles

Begin the exercise yourself. Be creative, yet specific, in the words you choose. When you're finished, have your group members follow suit.

Rate your week *10 min*

Hand out copies of **Rate Your Week** (page 115) and pencils. Instruct your group members to mark each line in the appropriate spot to indicate their personal ratings in that area for the previous week. Give them a minute or so to complete the handout. When they're finished, discuss the handout as a group, using questions like these.

- **Which area did you rate the lowest on your handout? Why?**
- **Which area did you rate the highest on your handout? Why?**
- **Which area did you have the most trouble rating? Why?**

Encourage your group members to share and explain their ratings.

So many questions, so little time 30 *min*

Hand out several index cards and a pencil to each group member. Instruct your kids to write one question they have about the opposite sex on each card. During this meeting and your next meeting you're going to try to answer many of the questions as a group.

To give your kids an idea of the kind of questions you're looking for, read some of the following questions to your kids.

Questions for guys
- **How important is dating to most high school guys?**
- **Why are so many guys not interested in serious relationships in high school?**
- **Do guys categorize girls by stereotypes?**
- **Do guys like girls who are smarter than they are?**
- **What do guys think of girls who smoke, party, or are sexually active?**
- **Do guys want girls to be the aggressive ones in starting relationships?**
- **Why is it so hard for guys to ask girls out?**
- **Why are guys so interested in sex?**
- **How should a girl politely say no to sex?**
- **Do most guys want to marry a virgin?**
- **Where do you draw the line when it comes to physical activity with a girl you like?**
- **What should a guy say if his girlfriend wants to have sex with him?**
- **How do guys get hurt in a relationship?**
- **What are guys most interested in when it comes to the opposite sex?**
- **What do guys talk about with their friends?**

Questions for girls
- **What does a girl really mean when she says she doesn't want to get serious?**
- **Should a guy and girl be good friends before they date?**
- **Why do some girls need a boyfriend all of the time?**
- **How important is the physical part of dating to girls?**

- When should a person say "I love you" in a relationship?
- Who should pay for dates?
- How can a guy know if a girl likes him?
- How would you feel if you found out your boyfriend was sexually active before he dated you?
- Where do you draw the line when it comes to physical activity with a guy you like?
- How old do you want to be when you get married?
- How much do girls talk and think about guys and sex?
- Do you and your parents have the same beliefs about sex and dating?
- What do girls talk about with their friends?

Questions for anyone to answer

- Who's more emotional—guys or girls?
- What stereotypes about guys or girls would you like to see destroyed?
- Why do people "fall out of love"?
- Can guys and girls be close friends without getting romantically involved?
- Can a guy and a gal be friends after breaking up?

Let your group members spread out around the room to give them some privacy while they work. Give them three to five minutes to come up with their questions. Assure them each writer's identity will be kept secret.

After you collect the cards, read through them and sort them into two piles. One pile should be questions that deal with relationships and general information about the opposite sex. The second pile should be questions that deal specifically with dating, sex, and romance. (Don't toss the cards after the meeting; you'll need them again.)

During the rest of this meeting, tackle the questions that deal with everything but dating and sex. (You'll be discussing those issues during your next meeting.) Encourage all of your group members to participate in the discussion. Get everyone's input in matters of the opposite sex.

Says you *10 min*

Wrap up your session by sharing a few Bible verses that might help your group members in their quest to develop healthy relationships with people of the opposite sex.

Finally, brothers, whatever is true, whatever is noble, whatever is right, whatever is pure, whatever is lovely, whatever is admirable—if anything is excellent or praiseworthy—think about such things.

—Philippians 4:8

Put to death, therefore, whatever belongs to your earthly nature: sexual immorality, impurity, lust, evil desires and greed, which is idolatry. But now you must rid yourselves of all such things as these: anger, rage, malice, slander, and filthy language from your lips. Therefore, as God's chosen people, holy and dearly loved, clothe yourselves with compassion, kindness, humility, gentleness and patience.

—Colossians 3:5, 8, 12

Read Philippians 4:8 and Colossians 3:5, 8, 12. Then say something like—

These are pretty clear instructions on how we're supposed to treat each other and how we're not supposed to treat each other. Friendship, especially friendship with people of the opposite sex, is one of God's greatest gifts on earth. As in every area of life, he's given us some pretty clear instructions to help us.

Briefly share a couple of your own experiences in learning about members of the opposite sex, preferably experiences that relate to Paul's instructions in Philippians and Colossians.

Close the meeting by asking your group members to share one or two ideas they'll be taking away from the meeting.

Rate Your Week

Place an X on each scale to represent how well your week went in each of the following categories.

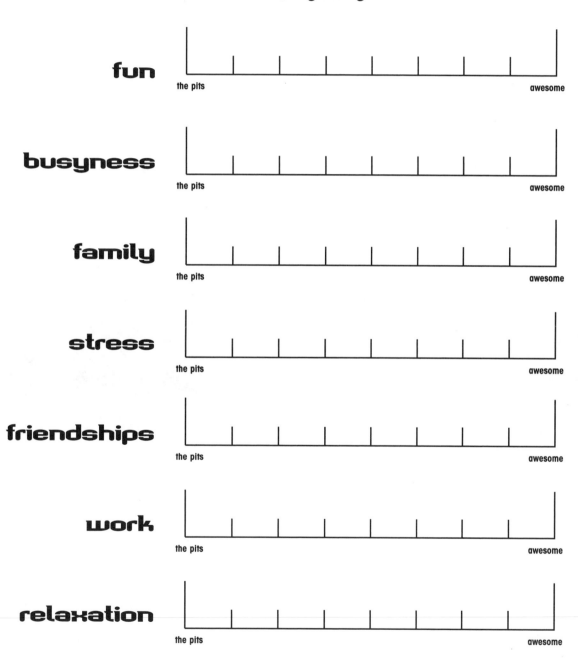

fun

the pits   awesome

busyness

the pits   awesome

family

the pits   awesome

stress

the pits   awesome

friendships

the pits   awesome

work

the pits   awesome

relaxation

the pits   awesome

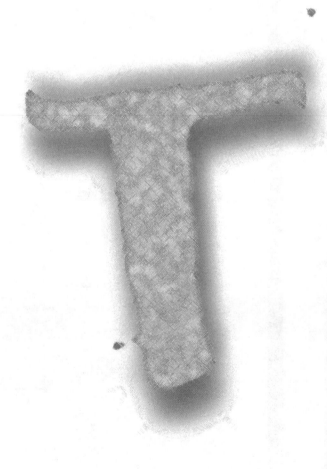

LET'S TALK about SEX & DATING

The purpose of this meeting is to challenge your group members to set God-pleasing personal standards in the areas of dating and sex.

In the beginning *15 min*

Begin by spending a few minutes catching up on each other's lives. You might want to do it this way—

I'll ask you to name a topic that has something to do with your life. It could be sports, your family, your boyfriend or girlfriend, homework, your job, your car, your favorite TV shows—whatever. After you name a topic, each of us will think of one question to ask you about that topic.

For this meeting you'll need...

- Question cards from the last meeting
- Bibles

You should be the first person on the hot seat. Name your topic and prepare yourself for your kids' questions. When you're finished, choose the next person to be grilled. Continue the process until everyone has been interviewed.

So many questions, so little time *30 min*

For this meeting you'll need the dating and sex question cards your group members wrote last week. Sort the dating and sex cards into three piles—questions for guys, questions for girls, and questions for the group in general. Whether you start with the guys or girls, draw a card from the appropriate pile and read the question. You may direct the question to one specific person or to the whole group of guys or girls.

After one group has answered a question, direct one to the other group, then throw out a question for the entire group. It's important for you to encourage honesty, vulnerability, and confidentiality among your group members throughout the activity. It's also important for you to maintain control of the discussion and prevent it from going off on any tangents. Continue until all of the questions have been answered.

Says you   10 min

Thank the kids for being so honest and open and let them know you respect them for their courage in sharing. Then say something like—

Some of the things we talked about don't have clear-cut answers. Those are the ones we need to pray about, to ask God for his input. Other areas of our discussion, though, are crystal clear—and the Bible has some interesting things to say about them.

Below you'll find some Bible verses and brief comments dealing with several different sexual issues. Read the verses; then customize the comments to fit your group's spiritual maturity level. Help your kids recognize that these are not merely suggestions for living a happy life; they are God's instructions on how he wants us to live.

Read (or ask some of your students to read) these passages:

- Galatians 5:19-21
- 1 Corinthians 6:13, 18
- Matthew 15:19

The acts of the sinful nature are obvious: sexual immorality, impurity and debauchery; idolatry and witchcraft; hatred, discord, jealousy, fits of rage, selfish ambition, dissensions, factions and envy; drunkenness, orgies, and the like. I warn you, as I did before, that those who live like this will not inherit the kingdom of God.
—Galatians 5:19-21

"Food for the stomach and the stomach for food"—but God will destroy them both. The body is not meant for sexual immorality, but for the Lord, and the Lord for the body. Flee from sexual immorality. All other sins a man commits are outside his body, but he who sins sexually sins against his own body.
—1 Corinthians 6:13, 18

For out of the heart come evil thoughts, murder, adultery, sexual immorality, theft, false testimony, slander.
—Matthew 15:19

Summarize whichever of the following points seem most appropriate for you and your small group, based on the Bible passages above:

- **Premarital sex is wrong according to God's Word.**

- **Adultery—that is, sex with someone other than your husband or wife—is wrong, according to God's Word.**

- **Premarital sex hurts relationships in many ways. It creates a dependence on physical acts for intimacy. It disrupts communication. It causes guilt, misunderstandings, and a lack of trust between partners.**

- **God gave us these instructions to protect us and help us have the best sexual experiences imaginable.**

- **The sexuality portrayed in the media, particularly in movies and on TV, is a dangerous lie. It deceives people into thinking that they can have consequence-free sex with people other than their spouses.**

- **The most important thing you can do for yourself is to set some specific personal standards regarding what you will and will not do sexually. You also need to be very clear about your reasons for those standards so that when you're tested, you'll be able to explain yourself.**

Finish the— *10 min*

Wrap up the session by asking your group members to complete these sentences openly and honestly.

- **One answer I will remember from this meeting is—**
- **One decision I've made—or need to make—about sex is—**
- **One thing I agree with from this meeting is—**

Encourage most of your group members to respond. Give a healthy dose of affirmation to those kids who have the courage to share their convictions and decisions with the entire group.

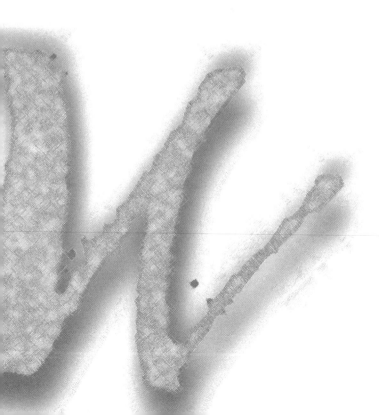

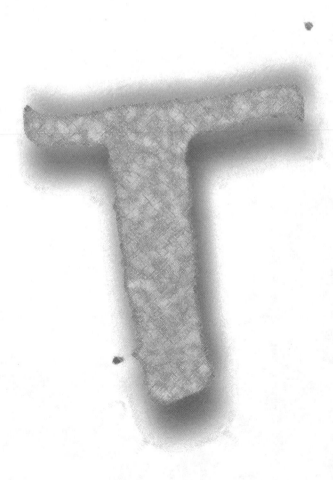

pressing CONCERNS

The purpose of this meeting is to help your group members evaluate their current and future priorities and commitments.

Stimuli *10 min*

Before the meeting, place some or all of these items in a bag: a picture of a homeless person, a picture of an attractive couple, a stuffed animal, a baby's toy, a personal family picture, a can of vegetables, a small Bible, a delicate flower, a T-shirt with a slogan on it, or items that might provoke reactions from your group members.

Split the group into pairs. (If at all possible, make them boy-girl pairs.)

When you pull an item out of the bag, your group members should each make a statement about the item to their partners. Let your kids know exactly what you're looking for in their statements by making a comment something like this—

For this meeting you'll need...

- A bag filled with some or all of the following items: a picture of a homeless person, a picture of an attractive couple, a stuffed animal, a baby's toy, a personal family picture, a can of vegetables, a small Bible, a delicate flower, and a T-shirt with a slogan in it
- Index cards
- Pencils
- Bibles
- Prepare some personal thoughts for "Says You" on page 123

> **When I show you an item, make sure that your discussion with your partner is personal and specific—and not just a general discussion about it. Try to begin most of your statements with phrases like, "I think," "I feel," "I want," or "I wish."**

After you've held up two or three items, mix up the partners. Continue until all of the items have been used.

Commitment papers *30 min*

Hand out index cards and pencils and instruct the kids to do two things—

On the front side of this card, I want you to make two lists. The first list should be the top five things you spend your time doing. The second list should be the top five things you spend your money on.

Some of your group members may try to claim that they have no money. If they do, remind them of the money their parents give them, birthday money, allowance, or the money they make from their job. Everyone spends some money!

Give the group about five minutes to make the two lists. Then say something like this—

On the back side of the card, I want you to make another list. This should be your top five priorities. In other words, I want you to list the five most important commitments in your life today.

It would probably be a good idea for you to share your own list of priorities at this point in order to get your group members thinking. Here are some examples you might consider.

1. To serve God faithfully
2. To be a loving spouse
3. To be a dedicated parent
4. To be a good teacher
5. To stay in good physical shape

Give your kids another five minutes to complete the final list. Begin the sharing portion of the activity by turning your card over and reading the first two lists you created.

Try to get some brief responses from the rest of the group by asking questions like these—

• Is anyone surprised by any of the items on this list?
• Do you notice any major differences between these two lists?

When you're finished, continue around the circle until everyone has read the first two lists and the group has responded. Then, ask them to turn the cards over and share their priority lists. Ask questions to clarify unclear priorities. After everyone has shared, put one more question to your kids—

If you were to begin living immediately according to the priorities on your list, what is one change you'd need to make in your life right now?

Answer the question yourself by revealing an area of needed change in your own life. Then have the group members respond.

Says you 5 min

Jesus had some hard words for those who call themselves Christians. Read Mark 8:34-37. Before your meeting think about what denying yourself, taking up a cross, and following Jesus means to you. Think about what it means to gain the whole world and what it means to lose your soul. Think about how you might apply these verses to your personal priority list. Briefly share with your group members some of the conclusions you reach.

Then he called the crowd to him along with his disciples and said: "If anyone would come after me, he must deny himself and take up his cross and follow me. For whoever wants to save his life will lose it, but whoever loses his life for me and for the gospel will save it. What good is it for a man to gain the whole world, yet forfeit his soul? Or what can a man give in exchange for his soul?"
—Mark 8:34-37

Compliments of the group 15 min

To wrap up the meeting, tell the group—

Let's make each other a priority as we close by focusing on each person here, and sharing some things that we like about each other. There are two guidelines for this exercise. When you give a compliment, make sure you look the person in the eyes. When you receive a compliment, either say "Thanks" or nothing at all. Don't ruin the compliment by denying its value.

After the compliment-fest, close your meeting in prayer, asking the Lord to help your group members live according to his priorities and his plans for their lives.

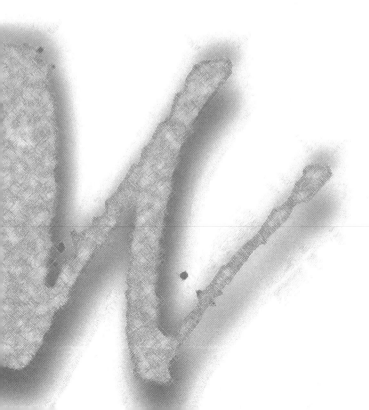

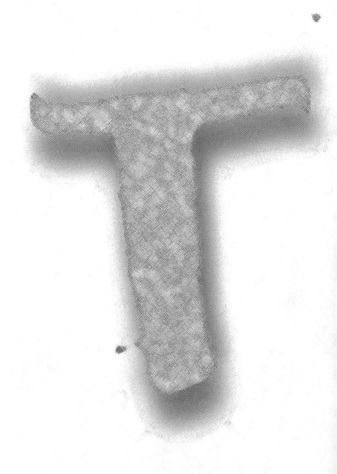

not perfect JUST FORGIVEN

The purpose of this meeting is to help your group members understand the importance of God's forgiveness and the importance of forgiving others.

In the beginning *10 min*

Start out the meeting by catching up on what's been going on this week. Give everyone one minute to update the group on events since the last time everyone was together. You go first, and then give everyone else a turn.

Listen closely to the things your group members share. You may find that some of them are struggling with some pretty serious issues. If that's the case in your group, waive the one-minute-per-person rule and spend some time comforting and encouraging those who are dealing with tough situations.

For this meeting you'll need...

- A copy of John 8:2-11 (page 131) for the Reader (optional)
- Bibles
- Prepare some personal thoughts about forgiveness for "Says You" on page 129

Visualize this *20 min*

Explain that the topic for this meeting is forgiveness—forgiving and being forgiven. The purpose of this activity is to help your kids think through the *effects* of forgiveness and to understand the *feelings* of persons in the Bible who experienced it.

First make some assignments. If you have fewer than six students, double up some parts; if you have more, let more than one student be in a role:

- *Reader* reads John 8:2-11 (from the Bible or from a copy of page 131), a few verses at a time (to allow for questions).
- *Jesus*
- *Woman*
- *Pharisees*
- *Disciples*
- *Bystanders*

Give the Reader a copy of page 131 or a Bible. Direct the reader to read verse 2, then ask the Bystanders the appropriate questions. Continue through the passage, prompting the reader, asking questions, and listening to students' responses. You can modify the questions, depending on your students' responses.

Reader:
[verse 2] At dawn he appeared again in the temple courts, where all the people gathered around him, and he sat down to teach them.

You, to the Bystanders:
   - **Why are you at the temple so early in the morning?**
   - **How are you feeling?**

Reader:
[verse 3] The teachers of the law and the Pharisees brought in a woman caught in adultery. They made her stand before the group…

You, to the Bystanders:
   - **What do you think of this interruption?**
   - **What do you think of this woman?**

You, to the Pharisees:
   - **Why did you bring her to Jesus?**

Reader:
[verses 4-5] …and said to Jesus, "Teacher, this woman was caught in the act of adultery. In the Law Moses commanded us to stone such women. Now what do you say?"

You, to the Bystanders:
   - **Now what do you think of this woman?**
   - **Where is the man who was with this woman? After all, you don't commit adultery by yourself!**

You, to Jesus:
   - **What do you think of this woman?**
   - **What do you think of the Pharisees?**
   - **Are you feeling any pressure at this point? Why (or why not)?**

You, to the Woman:
   - **What emotions are you experiencing at this point?**

Reader:

[verse 6] They were using this question as a trap, in order to have a basis for accusing him. But Jesus bent down and started to write on the ground with his finger.

You, to the Pharisees:
- **What do you think Jesus is writing?**
- **How do you feel now about bringing the woman to him?**
- **Do you think Jesus is on your side?**
- **What do you hope Jesus will do?**

You, to the Woman and the Bystanders:
- **How are you feeling at this point?**
- **What are you thinking?**

Reader:

[verses 7-8] When they kept on questioning him, he straightened up and said to them, "If any one of you is without sin, let him be the first to throw a stone at her." Again he stooped down and wrote on the ground.

You, to everyone:
- **What emotions are you experiencing at this point?**
- **Why did Jesus say what he did?**

Reader:

[verses 9-11] At this, those who heard began to go away one at a time, the older ones first, until only Jesus was left, with the woman still standing there. Jesus straightened up and asked her, "Woman, where are they? Has no one condemned you?" "No one, sir," she said. "Then neither do I condemn you," Jesus declared. "Go now and leave your life of sin."

You, to everyone except the Woman:
- **What did Jesus accomplish in this incident?**
- **Why didn't he have the Pharisees stone her?**
- **What do you disciples think of this event?**
- **Why did Jesus do what he did?**

You, to the entire group:
- **How do you think the woman responded to Jesus' forgiveness? Do you think she went back to committing adultery again the next day? Do you think she changed her life? If so, how—and why?**

A modern day parable *10 min*

Forgiveness is powerful. If you've experienced forgiveness, you may know what I mean. Let me tell you a modern-day parable that illustrates the power of forgiveness.

It was a Friday when your dad drove his first-ever brand new car into your driveway. Your whole family was excited, especially your mom. Your dad was as proud as you'd ever seen him when he escorted your mom to the car and then took her for a ride.

At supper that night you had an idea. Even though you knew he'd never let you do it, you asked anyway. "Dad, could I take the new car to the basketball game tonight?"

Your dad thought about how much he would have liked to drive a new car to one of his high school games. Much to your surprise, he agreed. "But just drive it to the game and then straight home," he said.

You gave him your word of honor.

When you got to the game you parked the car right out front where everyone could see it. Then you went inside and told your friends what you were driving. Of course they wanted a ride, but you said no because you remembered what you had promised your dad.

At halftime the person you've been dying to go out with forever walked over to you and said, "I heard you're driving a new car. I'd sure like a ride after the game!" Your brain melted. Your resistance vanished. You said, "No problem."

As it turned out, though, it wasn't just the two of you in the car after the game. Several friends piled in with you. And, as it turned out, it wasn't just a short ride. It was a ride across town to the pizza place.

When you came out of the restaurant, you knew you were in trouble. Everything was covered with ice. Sleet! You didn't get two blocks from the parking lot before you lost control of the car, sideswiped a telephone pole, and plowed into the side of another car. Your dad's new car was totally destroyed.

"Please just put me in jail!" you begged the police officers who came to investigate the accident. "I don't want to see my dad. He's going to tear me limb from limb." In spite of your pleas, the police called your dad and took you home.

When you reached the door of your house, you didn't want to go in. Your knees were knocking. You entered quietly, hoping your dad would be asleep.

He wasn't. He told you to come into the living room. You looked for something to protect yourself with.

When he turned to face you, you were terrified. After staring at you for a moment, he said, "I'm just glad you're not hurt. A car we can replace; a son we can't. Get a good night's sleep. Let's talk about it in the morning. I love you. Everything's okay."

You went upstairs and climbed into your bed. Then you cried.

What do you think of your father at this point?

Get a few responses from your group members; then continue.

The parable isn't over yet.

It's one week later. Your dad has purchased another new car. It's just like the last one. It's suppertime on Friday. Your family is eating together. Your dad reaches into his pocket and takes out the new set of car keys and hands them to you. He says, "I want you to take our new car to the game tonight."

How will you drive the car this time?

Get a few responses from your group members. You probably won't have to explain the truths of the parable to your kids, but you might want to be sure they've mentioned most of the following ideas—

You weren't punished for the first accident, yet you'll probably want to drive very carefully this time. Why is that? I think it's a demonstration of the power of forgiveness. I think it's also the same reason that the woman who was caught having an affair probably left her old life.

The awesome thing about being a Christian is that our heavenly Father gives us a brand new set of keys for life each and every day. And no matter what we did yesterday, if we are Christians, God gives us a clean, new start. That's forgiveness!

Finish the— *15 min*

The following sentence starters call for some serious reflection and openness on the part of your group members. Give a healthy dose of encouragement to the kids who have the guts to respond honestly to them.

- **One time someone needed to forgive me was when—**
- **I have trouble forgiving people when they—**
- **When someone totally forgives me, I feel—**
- **Someone I need to forgive right now is—**
- **One thing I need to ask God to forgive me for is—**

Says you *5 min*

Transition with thoughts like—

There are three words I want you to remember when it comes to forgiveness. They're pretty famous words, so you shouldn't have any trouble memorizing them.

Just do it. Just do it.

Whether you need to ask forgiveness from someone else or whether you need to forgive someone, just do it. The sooner, the better. You'll feel much better after you do.

For if you forgive men when they sin against you, your heavenly Father will also forgive you. But if you do not forgive men their sins, your Father will not forgive your sins.

—Matthew 6:14-15

Read Matthew 6:14-15. Briefly talk about the role forgiveness has played in your Christian life.

Check up *5 min*

Before you wrap up the meeting, divide your group into pairs. Ask your group members to take some time during the coming week to meet in person or talk by phone with their assigned partners, so they can encourage and support each other.

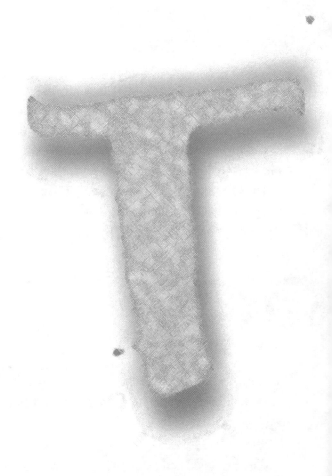

John 8:2-11

[verse 2]
At dawn he appeared again in the temple courts, where all the people gathered around him, and he sat down to teach them.

[verse 3]
The teachers of the law and the Pharisees brought in a woman caught in adultery. They made her stand before the group...

[verses 4-5]
...and said to Jesus, "Teacher, this woman was caught in the act of adultery. In the Law Moses commanded us to stone such women. Now what do you say?"

[verse 6]
They were using this question as a trap, in order to have a basis for accusing him. But Jesus bent down and started to write on the ground with his finger.

[verses 7-8]
When they kept on questioning him, he straightened up and said to them, "If any one of you is without sin, let him be the first to throw a stone at her." Again he stooped down and wrote on the ground.

[verses 9-11]
At this, those who heard began to go away one at a time, the older ones first, until only Jesus was left, with the woman still standing there. Jesus straightened up and asked her, "Woman, where are they? Has no one condemned you?" "No one, sir," she said. "Then neither do I condemn you," Jesus declared. "Go now and leave your life of sin."

who's ASKING?

The purpose of this meeting is to focus your group members' attention on some important questions about their lives.

So many questions, so little time *25 min*

Before the meeting starts, make a copy of **Questions, Questions, Questions** on page 136 and cut it into sections—one section for each person in your group. Make sure that each section has at least four questions on it. (If you have a large group, make two copies of the handout.)

As your group members arrive for the meeting, hand them a section of the handout. Explain the opening exercise by saying something like—

> **For this meeting you'll need...**
> • Copies of **Questions, Questions, Questions** (page 136)
> • Bibles

> Our topic today is questions—questions I have about you, questions you have about each other, and questions we all have about life in general. You'll notice that there are a few questions on the sheet I just gave you. For the first round of this activity, I want you to choose one of the questions on your handout to answer. I'll start.

Your openness and honesty will set an example for the rest of the group. That's why it's important not to shy away from tough answers. When you're finished answering your question, continue around the circle until everyone in the group has answered a question.

Then say something like—

> For the second round of this activity, I want you to choose a question from your handout for someone else in the group to answer. It may be

the question you just answered or one of the others. You can ask anyone in the group to answer it.

Choose one of the questions from your sheet and direct it to the group member of your choice. Give that person plenty of time to think about and then answer the question. The person who answers your question will then get to choose a question for someone else in the group. Go on until everyone has fielded a question.

For the third round of this activity, I want you to choose a question from your handout for the entire group to answer. Here's how it will work. You will read the question and then answer it yourself first. Then everyone else in the circle will answer it.

Encourage your group members to keep their responses brief during this round, so that you'll have time for everyone to ask a question.

Finish the— *5 min*

Before you move on give the kids a chance to ask some questions of their own.

I'll give you a couple of words, and I want you to ask the first question that pops into your head. Be honest, quick, spontaneous with your questions.

Use any of the following question starters or add your own ideas.

- **When will—**
- **How old will I be when—**
- **Why is—**
- **How does—**
- **Why are—**

Don't worry about trying to answer the questions—just have fun thinking of them.

Let's talk about you *20 min*

Now bring your discussion to a more personal level by asking your group members to answer questions that will reveal some things about their individual concerns, priorities, and interests. Give each member of your group a chance to answer each question.

Here are some questions you might use, if you feel they're appropriate for your group. If not, substitute some of your own ideas.

- If you could ask your parents one question about their past, what would you ask?
- If you could travel to heaven, stand in front of God, and ask God one question, what would you ask?
- If you could ask anyone in history one question, who would you choose and what would you ask?
- What one question would you like to answer to help your parents understand you better?
- If you could get one question answered about your future, what would you ask?

Says you *5 min*

Jesus asked some tough questions in the New Testament—the kind of questions that cause people to think long and hard about their lives. Some of the things he asked 2,000 years ago are questions we need to ask ourselves today. Have your kids imagine Jesus just walked into your room and started asking questions from the list below.

Direct each of the following questions to specific students in your group. After that person answers, open the floor for others to respond.

- Who do people say I am?
- Who do you say I am?
- Why are you so afraid? Do you still have no faith?

You may want to read Mark 4:35-41 or 8:27-30 with your group. Give students an opportunity to reflect on the questions again.

Did you hear that? *5 min*

You want your kids to believe that the personal information they've revealed during the meeting is important to the rest of the group, so try a listening activity to close.

Choose one person from the group to focus on at a time. Take turns recalling information you learned about the person during the meeting. Ideally, everyone in the group should contribute at least one recollection to the activity. If that doesn't happen, though, don't worry about it.

After you start the ball rolling with the first student, encourage your kids to recall some new personal information they learned about that person during the meeting. Continue until everyone has had a turn in the spotlight.

That day when evening came, he said to his disciples, "Let us go over to the other side." Leaving the crowd behind, they took him along, just as he was, in the boat. There were also other boats with him. A furious squall came up, and the waves broke over the boat, so that it was nearly swamped. Jesus was in the stern, sleeping on a cushion. The disciples woke him and said to him, "Teacher, don't you care if we drown?"

He got up, rebuked the wind and said to the waves, "Quiet! Be still!" Then the wind died down and it was completely calm.

He said to his disciples, "Why are you so afraid? Do you still have no faith?"

They were terrified and asked each other, "Who is this? Even the wind and the waves obey him!"

—Mark 4:35-41

Jesus and his disciples went on to the villages around Caesarea Philippi. On the way he asked them, "Who do people say I am?"

They replied, "Some say John the Baptist; others say Elijah; and still others, one of the prophets."

"But what about you?" he asked. "Who do you say I am?"

Peter answered, "You are the Christ."

Jesus warned them not to tell anyone about him.

—Mark 8:27-30

trade secret

If time gets tight at the end of your meeting, you may be tempted to skip this section. *Don't.* This activity is important because it helps kids recognize that the others in the group are actually paying attention to them.

Questions, Questions, Questions

From this list of questions choose the ones you think will best work with your group.

- What is one event from your past that you would like to watch again on videotape?
- What would life be like without friends?
- What do you dread?
- Who would you like to share an honest secret with?
- How do you feel when someone prays for you?
- If you were a food processor, what part would you be? Why?
- How would you react if your best friend hit your mom?
- Who was the first person who told you about sex? How did you respond? How did you feel?
- What was the worst small group meeting we ever had?
- Do you believe there is life on other planets? Why or why not?
- What is your favorite place at school? Why?
- Have you ever stolen anything? If so, what was it? When did you do it?
- What kinds of things do you like to read?
- Have you grown closer to God or farther away from him in the past 30 days?
- In what ways do you show honor and respect toward your parents?
- What do you worry about?
- What is one of your biggest temptations? How do you avoid giving in to it?
- Are you really angry at someone right now? If so, who? Why?
- When was the last time you were really hurt?
- Do you have a favorite photograph? If so, what is it?
- What is your favorite part of the newspaper? Why?
- What is your favorite way to travel? Why?
- Why is freedom important to you?
- When was the first time you kissed someone of the opposite sex? What did you think about it?
- What subject would you be most willing to argue about?
- What is one thing you would never want your parents to know about you?
- How do you feel about dancing?
- What would you like to do on a beautiful summer day?
- What was the last negative change in your life?
- Are you a moody person? What are your moods like?
- How much change do you need in your life to remain happy?
- How do you feel about pets? Wild animals?
- What is one of your funniest memories?
- How do you feel about people with religious views different from yours?
- What is your favorite game? Why?
- What is your favorite part of the Bible? Why?
- What are your thoughts about getting married in the future?
- What have you taught someone else about or taught them to do?

the substance of things HOPED FOR

The purpose of this meeting is to help your group members understand that faith means making choices every day to be on Jesus' team.

In the beginning *10 min*

Open up the meeting by sharing some of the things that have happened since the last time everyone was together. This time paint a picture with words to describe your answers. Be detailed. Here's a list of categories you might consider using. You may go through several.

For this meeting you'll need...

- Bibles
- Index cards
- Pencils

- **A time this week when I was stressed out**
- **A time this week when I was in trouble**
- **A time this week when I had fun with friends**
- **A time this week when I was relaxed**
- **A time this week when I was confused**
- **A time this week when I was happy**

Says you *10 min*

Now move into this meeting's topic. Since it can be hard to keep your arms around the concept of faith, start by defining it with your kids.

Anyone who knows me can tell you that my faith in Jesus is very important to me. As a matter of fact, it's the foundation of my life. But what is faith? We talk about it all the time, but do we really have any

idea what it means to have faith in someone or something? Let's see what the Bible says about it.

Read Romans 10:9-10. Call on a couple students to share what they think these verses tell us about faith. Though the kids may not give the responses you're looking for, it's important that you affirm any attempts at honest answers. Then read James 2:14-17. Ask questions like these—

- **What is the relationship between faith and good deeds?**
- **Is it possible to have faith without physically showing it?**
- **Is it possible to do good deeds for others without having faith?**

Encourage most, if not all, of your group members to offer their opinions. If you find that two or more of your kids disagree on the subject, let them debate for a few minutes, giving each side a chance to share its reasoning. This illustration may help—

I think faith is a little like falling in love and getting married. A love relationship focuses on one specific person. That person becomes your husband or wife. The faith we're talking about also focuses on one specific person. That person is Jesus, God's son.

The first step of the love-and-marriage process is finding out about a person. It's pretty hard to fall in love with someone you don't know. The first step toward faith is finding out the facts about Jesus.

The second step in the love-and-marriage process is believing in your heart that you're in love with the person. We just read in Romans that one of the steps toward faith is believing in your heart that God raised Jesus from the dead.

The third step in the love-and-marriage process is the actual event. Usually that involves taking vows and saying the words "I do" at a wedding ceremony. Legally you're not married until you say those words. One of the verses from Romans said that faith involves confessing with our mouths what we believe about Jesus.

Marriage is an everyday relationship that continues to grow all of the time. It involves living each day of your life as a married person. Faith in Christ is also an everyday relationship that continues to grow all of the time. It involves living each day as a Christian.

This would be an excellent time for you to share some information about your own personal faith, if you're comfortable doing so with your group.

Faith graphs   *25 min*

Hand out index cards and pencils. Explain that you and your group members will be making individual graphs to chart the development of your faith.

Instruct your group members to write numbers, representing the years of the Christian life, across the bottom of the card. For example, if a person became a Christian when he was seven, he should begin with seven and space the numbers evenly up to his current age. Continue with words like these—

That if you confess with your mouth, "Jesus is Lord," and believe in your heart that God raised him from the dead, you will be saved. For it is with your heart that you believe and are justified, and it is with your mouth that you confess and are saved.
—Romans 10:9-10

What good is it, my brothers, if a man claims to have faith but has no deeds? Can such faith save him? Suppose a brother or sister is without clothes and daily food. If one of you says to him, "Go, I wish you well; keep warm and well fed," but does nothing about his physical needs, what good is it? In the same way, faith by itself, if it is not accompanied by action, is dead.
—James 2:14-17

Starting with when you first began to believe in your heart that Jesus was raised from the dead, mark on your graph how committed you were to your faith. The higher your mark on your card, the greater your commitment.

Continue making marks for each year of your life since then, indicating how your commitment level has risen and fallen since then.

Ask your group members to put some serious thought into their graphs. Encourage them to recall the personal experiences and emotions that have impacted their faith over the years. Emphasize the importance of honesty and openness in this activity. Everyone's faith has ebbs and flows; your kids don't need to be ashamed of low places on their charts.

After your kids have plotted the vertical points on their graphs, instruct them to connect the dots with lines that show the ups and downs of their faith.

After giving your group members several minutes to work, begin the sharing process. One at a time, have students display their graphs to the entire group and reveal some of the events that influenced their faith positively and negatively over the years. Lead the way for your group by sharing and explaining your graph first.

trade secret
This activity calls for some risky sharing on the part of your group members. Be prepared to reward them with encouragement, appreciation, and affirmation. If you know there are non-Christians in the group, or suspect there are, acknowledge that there may be some kids who won't be participating in this graph and that they shouldn't feel badly about it.

Picture this *15 min*

Before ending this meeting, guide the group back to the word-picture exercise done earlier in the session.

I want each of you to give us a detailed description of what you picture when you think of each category. Remember to be as creative and specific as possible when you share.

To give your kids an idea of what you're looking for, share your own word picture first for each category. Be very specific, using as much detail as possible to describe the images and feelings you experience.
Use any or all of the following categories, or make up your own.

- **Share a picture of where you are and how you feel when you're close to God.**
- **Share your favorite picture of Jesus from the Bible.**
- **Share your picture of a committed Christian who is serving God.**
- **Share a picture of where you are and what you're doing when you're living your faith.**

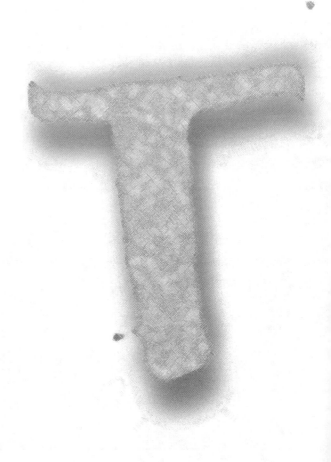

growing UP

The purpose of this meeting is to help your group members identify and examine the various doors to adulthood through which they must pass.

In the beginning *10 min*

Divide your kids into groups of three. Give each trio two minutes to focus on one person in the group. The other two people should ask as many questions as they can think of in those two minutes, focusing specifically on the things that occurred in the person's life in the past week. When time is up, allow a minute or so for each group to briefly report on what was learned.

> Repeat the process two more times, so each group member gets her turn in the spotlight. It's important that you keep this activity moving at a brisk pace.

For this meeting you'll need...

- Blank sheets of paper, prepared according to the instructions on page 143
- Marker
- Bibles

Thinkin' and feelin' *20 min*

Transition by asking the kids something along this line—

When was the last time someone told you to grow up?

Get a few responses from your kids. Ask them to include as many details as they're comfortable sharing. Who said it to them? What were the circumstances? Were they really acting childish? How did they feel about being told to grow up? Then continue.

It just so happens that the topic of our meeting today is growing up—the path to adulthood. Before we start talking about grown-up things, though, I want to do a quick exercise. I want you to begin practicing the skill of separating your thoughts from your feelings.

It may sound like an easy thing to do, but it's not. I'm going to read three different situations, and I want you to share your thoughts and feelings about each one.

Situation 1—You drive your family's car to a nearby store after taking it through a car wash. When you come out of the store, you notice that the entire driver's side of the car is smashed. It looks like someone ran into it going 50 miles an hour. The damage is really bad. What are some things you might be *thinking?*

Listen closely to the statements your kids give you. Make sure that they are indeed statements of thought—that is, practical and nonemotional thoughts. Then ask—

How might you be *feeling* as you look at the damaged car?

This will likely be the harder of the two questions. Pay attention to the words your group members use to describe their feelings—words such as sad, frustrated, scared, angry, or numb. Continue, perhaps with questions like—

Is it more difficult for you to give thinking statements or feeling statements? Why?

Encourage group members to respond. Now go to the second scenario.

Situation 2—Life is good for you. You live in a big house in a nice neighborhood in a good city. You've got great friends and attend a really cool high school. Your classes are going great, your grades are high, and your extracurricular calendar is full. It's good to be you. And then your dad makes his announcement. It seems that his company has transferred him to a different region of the country. You and your family will be moving to a city over 1,000 miles away. Oh, and there's one more thing. You'll be leaving in three days. What are your thoughts?

Again make sure that your kids don't give you feeling statements disguised as thinking statements. The two are easy to confuse. After some discussion, ask—

What are your feelings? How difficult is it for you to separate your thoughts and feelings in this situation?

Let the group talk about that for a few minutes, then introduce Situation 3.

Situation 3—It's your birthday. You have some friends come to your house for a small party. Some of them bring gifts. One of the gifts is a book of five lottery tickets. During the party you watch the lottery drawing on TV to see if any of your tickets are winners. You stare in amazement as the numbers flash across the screen. One of your tickets matches all six numbers! You're the grand prize winner—the owner of a ticket worth more than $10 million! What are you thinking? What are you feeling?

Note the differences between the way your kids think and the way they feel. Wrap up the activity by briefly discussing the general differences between thoughts and feelings, as well as the role that each type plays in a person's life.

The doors *25 min*

Before the session you'll need to prepare several blank sheets of paper by folding them in half twice (so it looks like a small book). The sheets of paper represent doors to adulthood.

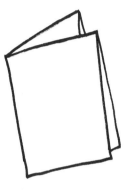

Becoming an adult is like walking through an indoor maze. You have to pass through quite a few doors before you finally reach your destination. Let's think about some of the doors that lead to adulthood.

Ask your group members to help you think of some rites of passage that are necessary for kids who want to be treated like adults. After each suggestion is offered, write it on one of the sheets of paper and then stand that sheet in the middle of the group.

You may need to offer some suggestions to get your group members' creative juices flowing. Here's a partial list of doors to adulthood.

- **Celebrating your 18th (or 21st) birthday**
- **Becoming financially independent**
- **Establishing your freedom from your parents' control**
- **Becoming successful in a career**
- **Graduating from high school (or college)**
- **Gaining the respect of other adults**
- **Living in your own home**
- **Getting married**
- **Making adult decisions**

After you've placed several paper doors in the middle of the group, have your kids take turns choosing a door and talking about their thoughts—not their feelings—concerning that rite of passage.

Start things off yourself by choosing a door and talking about your experiences in trying to pass through it.

For the second round of this activity, ask your group members to choose a door and talk about their feelings concerning that rite of passage. Encourage your kids to be open and honest in the feelings they share.

Says you *5 min*

The thought of becoming an adult may seem fun, scary, frustrating, unsettling, or exciting, depending on the circumstances. Tell the kids you know a Bible verse that may help them when their thoughts and feelings about the future start to be overwhelming.

Read 2 Corinthians 4:18 two times so your group members get the full effect of the verse. After you read it the second time, ask your group members to share their thoughts and feelings about the verse.

You may want to assist your kids by giving them one of the following statements to complete.

- **I think the verse is—**
- **I think the key word in the verse is—**
- **I think the verse is important because—**
- **As I listened to the verse I felt—**
- **The idea of eternity makes me feel—**

Close the meeting by sharing some of your personal thoughts and feelings about things that are seen and temporary (as opposed to unseen and eternal).

So we fix our eyes not on what is seen, but on what is unseen. For what is seen is temporary, but what is unseen is eternal.
—2 Corinthians 4:18

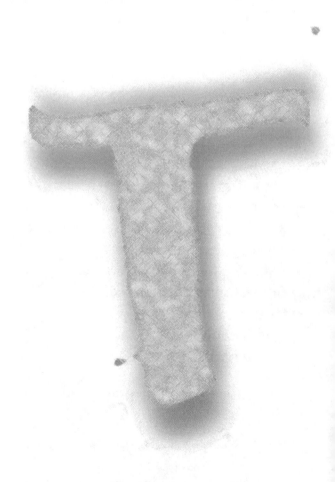

encouraging SIGNS

The purpose of this meeting is to help your group members learn to encourage each other.

Trust me *10 min*

Begin your meeting with an experiment in trust. Ask for a volunteer to serve as a test subject. This person should select two people whom he considers to be trustworthy from your group. Those two people should stand facing each other, just behind the volunteer.

In this trust experiment, the volunteer must fall backward into the arms of the two people he selected. To demonstrate his trust, the volunteer must keep his arms and legs perfectly straight as he falls and not try to catch himself or break his fall.

Obviously the role of the other two group members is to catch the volunteer. Just to be safe, you may want to emphasize the importance of not dropping the volunteer. Then emphasize it again, just to be extra cautious.

Assuming that everything goes well with the first trust fall, bring up a few more trios from the group to try the experiment. Pay attention to which group members seem to trust their catchers and which ones try to break their falls.

> **For this meeting you'll need...**
>
> - Create a simple obstacle course according to the directions on page 146
> - Copies of **How I See Myself** (page 149)
> - Pencils
> - Bibles

trade secret
Some group members who are self-conscious about their weight or appearance may be uncomfortable with this activity. Respect their feelings. Don't force anyone to participate in this activity.

Walk this way *5 min*

Divide your group into pairs for a second experiment in trust. Explain the activity to the pairs—

One of you must close your eyes and keep them closed throughout the entire exercise. Your partner will be giving you verbal directions to help you move around. Those of you giving directions may not touch your partner at all. Those of you with your eyes closed will show how much you trust your partner by doing the things your partner says. Those of you who are giving directions will prove your trustworthiness by not letting your partner run into anything.

One of the keys to success in this activity is choosing a good course for the pairs to travel. If possible, plan a route that takes your group members outside, around a tree, up a flight of stairs, through a few doorways, and so on.

After all of the pairs have completed the course, lead your group in a brief discussion of the two trust experiments. Use the following questions to get things started, if necessary—

- **Which of these activities required the most trust? Why?**
- **Did you ever worry that the people you trusted might let you down? Why or why not?**
- **How much do you trust the people in this group?**
- **What are some ways people can prove they're trustworthy?**

Let's talk about me 15 min

Hand out copies of **How I See Myself** (page 149) and pencils. Instruct your group members to mark an X on each line to indicate where they fit in each category.

After everyone has finished, divide the group into pairs. Have your kids explain their marks for the first two lines. Why did they mark where they did on the line? How different are their responses from their partners'?

After a couple of minutes, have group members switch partners and explain their marks for the third and fourth lines. Continue switching partners and sharing until all of the lines on the handout have been discussed.

Wrap up the exercise by pointing out that sharing personal information with other people is a way of building trust. We rely on those people not to use the information against us. Suggest also that sharing personal information with another person opens the door for a supportive and encouraging relationship.

Finish the— 10 min

Bring your group members back together in a circle for the now-familiar exercise of finishing sentences that you read. Encourage your kids to be honest and open in their answers—assuming, of course, that they choose to answer. They always have the option of declining to respond.

Explain that the sentence starters are designed to get your kids talking about themselves. You can either use the suggestions below or come up with some of your own.

- One thing that my mom or dad has done to encourage me is—
- One thing that a teacher has done to encourage me is—
- One thing that a friend has done to encourage me is—
- I feel most encouraged when—
- Discouragement often hits me when—
- To fight discouragement, I usually—
- God encourages me because—

Says you *5 min*

Have the group members imagine everyone they meet is carrying a big bucket that holds water. In this case, though, the water represents encouragement. So people who are very discouraged have buckets that are almost empty. They need water desperately. On the other hand, people who are happy and encouraged have buckets overflowing with water. Say something like—

Every time we run into people or spend time with them, we have the opportunity either to put water into their bucket or take it out. It seems like some people are always dipping into someone else's bucket and taking their water by discouraging them. Other people are always ready to scoop some of their water into your bucket just to encourage you. Those people are supportive and fun to be with.

God is the greatest encourager of all. He's an endless source of water. As a matter of fact, he loaded the Bible with verses of tremendous encouragement for people who love him. Let me read just a few of those verses to you right now.

Read Romans 8:34-39.
　　As a group discuss ways these verses can be an encouragement to you and your group members. Use questions like the following to guide your discussion.

- **Why is it impossible for anything to separate us from the Lord's love?**
- **How does it make you feel to know that the Lord is always with you, no matter what you're facing?**
- **How would you explain these verses to someone in serious need of encouragement?**

Who is he that condemns? Christ Jesus, who died—more than that, who was raised to life—is at the right hand of God and is also interceding for us. Who shall separate us from the love of Christ? Shall trouble or hardship or persecution or famine or nakedness or danger or sword? As it is written: "For your sake we face death all day long; we are considered as sheep to be slaughtered." No, in all these things we are more than conquerors through him who loved us. For I am convinced that neither death nor life, neither angels nor demons, neither the present nor the future, nor any powers, neither height nor depth, nor anything else in all creation, will be able to separate us from the love of God that is in Christ Jesus our Lord.

—Romans 8:34-39

Encouragement practice *15 min*

Divide your group members into pairs for this final exercise. Tell the kids the time for talking is done. Now it's time to start practicing encouragement. For the next few minutes, you want them and their partners to do nothing but encourage each other. They may need suggestions like these—

If you're wondering what that means, keep in mind that smiles are encouraging, hugs are encouraging, words are encouraging, and listening is encouraging.

You may be uncomfortable at first, but that will pass. Just think about the kinds of things that encourage you, and do them for your partner. When I give the signal to switch, find a different partner and encourage her until I have you switch again. We'll do this five times.

If you have an odd number of kids, join in the activity yourself to even things out.

At the end of the session, ask your group members to continue their encouraging ways outside of your meeting time. Ask them to make contact with one or more people from the group in the coming week and offer encouragement in the form of a phone call, a hug, a note, or an invitation to McDonald's.

How I See Myself

Indicate where you fit into each category by marking the appropriate spot on each line (least to most, left to right).

[LEVEL OF PHYSICAL ACTIVITY]

Your idea of *active* is walking the empty pizza box from the TV to the kitchen garbage can

Cut P.E. only once a term

Always park at the far end of the mall lot just so you can walk the quarter mile to the stores

[INTROVERT VS. EXTROVERT]

Chatrooms are your idea of socializing

Lunchtime with a few friends is the high point of your day

Solitude drives you nuts—to talk is to live

[TOLERANCE]

There's *nothing* your friends could do that would kill your friendship

You don't usually flip out about things you don't agree with

You are God's instrument of judgment on those who mess up

[ANY FRIENDS?]

Lonely Hearts Club

Three's Company

The Roar of the Crowd

[HOW IMPORTANT ARE *THINGS* TO YOU?]

I dwell in the realm of ideas and relationships

Actually, an iMac would sure help keep up those relationships

Give me a BMW and a season pass to Aspen, or give me death

[DEGREE OF FAITH]

You just renewed your membership in the Society of Atheists

Church is great, youth group is fun, and so are the girls there

You need God like you need water, and when God tells you to jump, your only question will be, "How high?"

[ACADEMIC MOTIVATION]

School is a farce, and the sooner you're out, the better

Good grades are okay, but why knock yourself out for straight A's?

Must must *must* be accepted into Stanford or Harvard

the TRUTH about MOODS

The purpose of this meeting is to help your group members learn to examine their moods and consider ways to manage them.

Video Stars *(15 minutes)*

Introduce your teens to the meeting topic with comments like these—

Imagine that your entire life has been recorded on video and that we have the tape here today. Think about it: every single minute of your life on one tape. Now imagine that we want to find the "extreme" moments in your life—the times when you were really, really happy, sad, angry, afraid, or depressed. Which extreme mood do you think would be easiest for us to find? Why?

For this meeting you'll need...
- Blankets (one per person)
- Candles or fireplace and log, matches (optional)
- Bibles

Share thoughts about your own life first. Give the kids opportunities to share. Then let teens answer one or two of the following questions. You can pick the question randomly for each student or read the questions off and let students choose.

- **Which other extreme moods are most common to you? Why do you suppose that is?**
- **Which extreme moods would be hardest to find on your tape? Why?**
- **What has made you extremely happy? Sad? Angry? Afraid? Depressed?**

On reaching Jerusalem, Jesus entered the temple area and began driving out those who were buying and selling there. He overturned the tables of the money changers and the benches of those selling doves and would not allow anyone to carry merchandise through the temple courts. And as he taught them, he said, "Is it not written: 'My house will be called a house of prayer for all nations'? But you have made it 'a den of robbers.'"

The chief priests and the teachers of the law heard this and began looking for a way to kill him, for they feared him, because the whole crowd was amazed at his teaching.

—Mark 11:15-18

Now a man named Lazarus was sick. He was from Bethany, the village of Mary and her sister Martha. This Mary, whose brother Lazarus now lay sick, was the same one who poured perfume on the Lord and wiped his feet with her hair. So the sisters sent word to Jesus, "Lord, the one you love is sick."

When he heard this, Jesus said, "This sickness will not end in death. No, it is for God's glory so that God's Son may be glorified through it." Jesus loved Martha and her sister and Lazarus. Yet when he heard that Lazarus was sick, he stayed where he was two more days.

Then he said to his disciples, "Let us go back to Judea."

"But Rabbi," they said, "a short while ago the Jews tried to stone you, and yet you are going back there?"

Jesus answered, "Are there not twelve hours of daylight? A man who walks by day will not stumble, for he sees by this world's light. It is when he walks by night that he stumbles, for he has no light."

After he had said this, he went on to tell them, "Our friend Lazarus has fallen asleep; but I am going there to wake him up."

His disciples replied, "Lord, if he sleeps, he will get better." Jesus had been speaking of his death, but his disciples thought he meant natural sleep.

So then he told them plainly, "Lazarus is dead, and for your sake I am glad I was not there, so that you may believe. But let us go to him."

Then Thomas (called Didymus) said to the rest of the disciples, "Let us also go, that we may die with him."

On his arrival, Jesus found that Lazarus had already been in the tomb for four days. Bethany was less than two miles from Jerusalem, and many Jews had come to Martha and Mary to comfort them in the loss of their brother. When Martha heard that Jesus was coming, she went out to meet him, but Mary stayed at home.

"Lord," Martha said to Jesus, "if you had been

- Do you consider yourself a moody person? Why or why not?
- Do you think there's anything wrong with being moody? Why or why not?

The Life and Times of Jesus *(10 minutes)*

Transition by saying—

What if we had a video of the life of Jesus? I'm talking about an actual tape shot during his lifetime. What kind of moods do you think we might see on it? Do you think the Son of God ever got really happy or sad or angry or afraid or depressed?

Use any or all of the following questions to continue your discussion:

- **If Jesus lived as a human being like us, does that mean he experienced all the feelings and emotions we experience?**
- **How do you think Jesus might have handled his moods differently than the way we handle ours? Why?**
- **When you picture Jesus in your mind, what kind of mood is he in?**
- **What do you think would surprise most people about Jesus' earthly life?**

Says You *(10 minutes)*

Share some thoughts like these with your students.

Some writers of the New Testament knew it would be important to keep a historical account of the life of Jesus. That's why they recorded the events of his life as best they could. Of course, they didn't have video cameras back then, so they had to use words. Let's take a look at just a couple of the things they recorded.

Have someone read Mark 11:15-18.

How would you describe Jesus' mood in these verses? What do you think caused his mood?

Listen to student ideas. Have other students read John 11:1-37.

How would you describe Jesus' mood in this passage? What do you think caused his mood?

After you've heard your teens' ideas, say—

I want to read one more verse. Listen closely to see what it says to us about our own moods.

Read Ephesians 4:26.

What does this verse tell us about our emotions?

If no one else mentions it, point out that it suggests we can have bad moods—we can even get angry—and still not sin. The key is how we *deal* with our moods and emotions.

Get several different reactions from your group members before moving on to the final section of the lesson.

Mood Change *25 min*

While we're talking about moods, I want to change the mood of our group right now.

Hand out blankets to your group members to use in whatever way they choose. Some kids may use their blankets as pillows. Others may cover up with them. Someone may use it more creatively.

Turn out the lights in the room and draw the blinds or curtains on the windows. If possible, light a couple of candles—or perhaps even a fireplace.

I hope this changes the mood of our group a little and makes it easier to think about the different moods we go through. At least the blankets will make us feel more cozy.

Spend the final part of your meeting asking your group members to complete the following sentences. Use the ones you think will work best for your group—the ones that will motivate your kids to open up about their personal moodiness.

- **One thing that really affects my moods is—**
- **The mood that I dislike in myself the most is—**
- **My moods affect other people when—**
- **One thing that helps me control my moods is—**
- **Turning out the lights and lighting candles affects my mood by—**

here, my brother would not have died. But I know that even now God will give you whatever you ask."

Jesus said to her, "Your brother will rise again."

Martha answered, "I know he will rise again in the resurrection at the last day."

Jesus said to her, "I am the resurrection and the life. He who believes in me will live, even though he dies; and whoever lives and believes in me will never die. Do you believe this?"

"Yes, Lord," she told him, "I believe that you are the Christ, the Son of God, who was to come into the world."

And after she had said this, she went back and called her sister Mary aside. "The Teacher is here," she said, "and is asking for you." When Mary heard this, she got up quickly and went to him. Now Jesus had not yet entered the village, but was still at the place where Martha had met him. When the Jews who had been with Mary in the house, comforting her, noticed how quickly she got up and went out, they followed her, supposing she was going to the tomb to mourn there.

When Mary reached the place where Jesus was and saw him, she fell at his feet and said, "Lord, if you had been here, my brother would not have died."

When Jesus saw her weeping, and the Jews who had come along with her also weeping, he was deeply moved in spirit and troubled. "Where have you laid him?" he asked.

"Come and see, Lord," they replied.

Jesus wept.

Then the Jews said, "See how he loved him!"

But some of them said, "Could not he who opened the eyes of the blind man have kept this man from dying?"

—John 11:1-37

In your anger do not sin: Do not let the sun go down while you are still angry.

—Ephesians 4:26

153

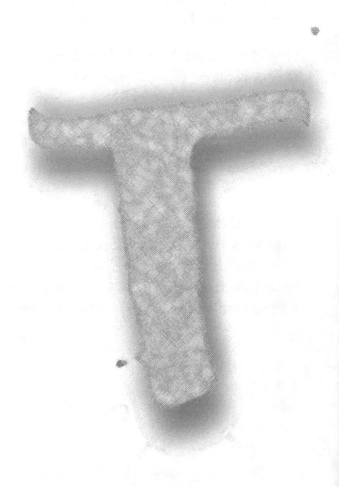

a friend IN NEED

The purpose of this meeting is to help your group members improve their abilities to help their friends in times of need.

Extra! Extra! Read all about it! *15 min*

Hold up a newspaper for your group members to see. Quickly go through the various sections of the paper, selecting a few headlines to read from each one. Say something like the following—

For this meeting you'll need...

• A newspaper

> **What if this newspaper had been covering the events in your life during the past week? What would some of the headlines say? Remember, we're not just talking about one section of the paper; we're talking about the whole thing.**
>
> **For example, what would be the headline on the front page? Remember, the biggest, most important news events are found on that page. So what's the most important, newsworthy event that happened in your life during the past week?**

Start things off by sharing a front-page headline from your own life. Briefly talk about a few details of the event, but don't get too caught up in it. After you share, encourage the rest of the group to do the same.

Then move on to some other sections of the paper. Here's a list of possibilities.

• **Sports section—news about your workouts or an important game**

• **Family section—news about your parents, siblings, or home life in general**

- Entertainment section—news about what movie you saw, a favorite TV show, or a new song
- Advice column—a problem or unresolved issue you know you could use help with
- Financial section—news about a new job or a decision about career plans
- Religion section—news about something you learned about God or a memorable church event

Either / or *10 min*

So far you've gathered facts. Now tell the group members you're going to talk about feelings.

Here's what we'll do. I'm going to give you two different feelings to choose from. I want you to choose the one that you felt more strongly during the week since we last met and then explain why you experienced it.

Read each of the following sets of words, giving your kids plenty of time to respond to each set. Encourage your group members to share as much information about their feelings as they're comfortable with.

If you can think of your own sets of words for this activity, feel free to add them to the list below.

- **Excited...Bored**
- **Frustrated...Peaceful**
- **Angry...Grateful**
- **Intense...Laid back**
- **Happy...Sad**

Help for helpers *25 min*

The following passage is a collection of ideas concerning how to help friends in need. For maximum effectiveness, though, you'll need to put the ideas into your own words when you present this material to your group.

Talk with the kids about how friendship is one of the greatest gifts God gives us here on earth. Friends are a vital part of any happy, healthy life. Then explain that it's important to remember that friendship is a two-way street.

Being a good friend is every bit as important as having a good friend. One of the keys to being a good friend is being prepared to help a friend in need.

Helping a friend does not mean simply giving your advice when a problem pops up. Anyone can give advice. Your friend may need more from you—like help in finding a way to solve the problem. After all, he knows better than anyone what he's feeling and how he wants things to turn out.

List some steps they can take to help a friend help himself.

Let's consider some ways you can help your friends help themselves. Listen actively. This means letting your friend know—without even using words—that you're interested in listening to his problem and helping him. Some of you are excellent active listeners already. You use your face and your body to tell people that you're ready to listen.

Demonstrate a body position and facial expression that communicates the message that you don't care about listening. Then demonstrate a body position and facial expression that communicates an eagerness to listen.

Discuss as a group the subtle—but important—differences between the two postures. An eagerness to listen encourages people to keep talking and to continue working through their problems.

Quickly divide the group into pairs. Name a topic and ask one person in each pair to talk about it while the other person actively listens. After a short time, the partners should switch roles. (If you're looking for a provocative topic, try PROBLEMS WITH THE OPPOSITE SEX.)

After a few minutes bring the group back together and ask your kids to talk about the things their partners did to show they were listening. Then move on to the next step.

Show a willingness to understand. This is an important part of helping your friend continue to talk, think, and evaluate the problem. This doesn't mean that you keep saying, "I understand," over and over again. It means that you give feedback that proves you want to understand. To do this you must listen very closely for both facts and feelings. Your words will either tell your friend that you're listening closely or that you're not willing to work hard enough to really understand. You must listen to understand the problem from his point of view and not your own.

Quickly demonstrate this skill by listening and responding while one of your group members talks about some topic—say, unreasonable demands parents make. After a couple of minutes, stop the exercise and ask your kids what they observed in your attempt to understand.

If you have time, ask your kids to reassemble into the pairs they formed earlier. Give them a minute or two to practice communicating that they're listening to and trying to understand each other. Then continue.

Find out what part your friend played in creating the problem and what her goal is for solving it. It's important that you help your friend recognize her responsibility for the problem. Don't tell her what she did; ask questions to help her find out for herself. Remind yourself, too, that your friend's problem is just that—her problem. Don't try to take too much responsibility on yourself.

Then go to the fourth step.

Expand your friend's list of possible options and help him develop a step-by-step action plan for solving the problem. Many times people with problems are not able to see all of their options. By listening closely and letting your friend know you understand what's going on, you will be helping him develop new options.

Point out to your group members that they shouldn't expect to learn all of these steps at one time. Instead, they should simply take this opportunity to begin thinking about new ways of helping friends in need.

The ultimate help *10 min*

Wind up the meeting with your own words along these lines—

Helping friends solve everyday problems is important, but helping friends with faith in Jesus Christ is vital. I try to do both kinds of helping with my friends. And since I consider you guys my friends, I want to help you any way I can. If you need help with a problem, I would consider it a privilege to meet with you and help you work through your possible solutions.

If you want to do some thinking, praying, or talking about your Christian faith, I would also like to help you with that. I would love to meet with you to continue answering your questions or help you evaluate what you believe. If you're not sure about your decision, let's get together this week to talk.

Wrap up your session by reviewing the things your group members will be taking away from the meeting. Ask them to complete the following sentences.

- **The most important thing I learned in this meeting was—**
- **One thing I need to do to help my friends in need is—**

ALL GOOD THINGS must come to an END

The purpose of this meeting is to provide a positive conclusion to your kids' small group experience.

In the beginning *5 min*

Every small group eventually breaks up. There are many different reasons for concluding a small group experience. Regardless of the reasons your group is ending, it's important to conclude with a celebration of what your kids have meant to each other rather than just allowing things to peter out.

From the start of this meeting though, you need to emphasize the fact that while small groups end, friendships can go on forever.

Bring to the meeting a disposable paper cup and a valuable possession. Hold both items up for the group to see, and say something like this—

I want us to spend a few minutes thinking about our group. As you know, this is our last meeting.

Share honestly about what your group has meant to you and how you feel about ending your meetings together.

I want all of you to think of our group as a valuable possession rather than a paper cup. We live in a throwaway world. Almost everything we touch is disposable. It lasts for a while, but then we toss it away as unimportant or useless. This includes everything from cars to toys to books to anything else you can think of. Some people even think that

For this meeting you'll need...

- A paper cup
- A valued possession
- Bibles
- Special refreshments, parting gifts, or whatever you'd like to celebrate the finale with

trade secret
Since this will probably be a short meeting, you may want to plan to have an extended time of socializing at the end of your meeting.

friendships are a throwaway commodity. I don't! I don't want our group to be represented by this cup.

Tear up the cup and throw it on the floor.

I want you to think of this group and the memories of our time together as a possession you value, like this.

Hold up your valued possession and explain what it means to you.

Finish the— *15 min*

Remind the kids that in many of your meetings, you've talked to each other by finishing sentences.

Sometimes it helps us get started and sometimes it gets in the way. I have some sentences for us to finish, but if you think of something else you want to say, you can just go ahead and say it, even if it doesn't fit the sentence.

Some sentence starters you might want to use are—

- **One way this group has been fun for me is—**
- **One way this group has been important to me is—**
- **One thing I've learned from the group is—**
- **One thing I'll always remember about this group is—**
- **One feeling I've had about this last meeting is—**

Individual attention *15 min*

Choose one person from the group to focus on at a time. You and your kids should then take turns expressing positive feelings and affirmations to that person.

See to it that everyone in the group contributes at least one comment. To start the exercise, say something like this—

Jamael, you've grown by leaps and bounds in the time we've been meeting together. During our first few meetings, you barely said a word. Now I consider you one of the discussion leaders of this group. I'm really proud of you.

After you've shared, allow the others to comment. When everyone has shared about the first person, choose another. Continue until everyone has had a turn in the spotlight.

Says you *10 min*

Let your group members know you would love to stay in contact with them and hear from them on a regular basis throughout their lives. Be positive about the strength of the friendships you've developed. Then say something like this—

> **When you think of this group two months, 12 months, or five years from now, I hope that many of the things we've talked about are still with you. Above all else, though, there is one thing that I want you to remember forever. I want you remember the ideas in these five verses.**

Read 2 Corinthians 5:17-21.

> **These verses call us to be reconciled to God through Christ. That means to renew the relationship that was ruined by sin. These verses also call us to be ambassadors for Christ. That means when people see the things we do and hear the things we talk about, they should automatically associate us with Jesus. Never forget these two responsibilities. Each of you has unbelievable potential. I'm sure you will do some outstanding things in your lives. As you become successful, though, keep in mind that your most important responsibility is to live your lives as committed followers of Jesus Christ. Work to strengthen that commitment every day of your life, and you'll never have to worry what the future holds.**

> *Therefore, if anyone is in Christ, he is a new creation; the old has gone, the new has come! All this is from God, who reconciled us to himself through Christ and gave us the ministry of reconciliation: that God was reconciling the world to himself in Christ, not counting men's sins against them. And he has committed to us the message of reconciliation. We are therefore Christ's ambassadors, as though God were making his appeal through us. We implore you on Christ's behalf: Be reconciled to God. God made him who had no sin to be sin for us, so that in him we might become the righteousness of God.*
>
> —2 Corinthians 5:17-21

A final prayer *5 min*

What better way is there to end your last official group meeting than by praying for your group members?

Pray that—
- **Your group members will remember what they've learned in these sessions.**
- **The friendships they made in the group will last.**
- **God will continue to work in your kids' lives.**
- **Your group members will find other Christian friends to encourage them throughout their lives.**

notes

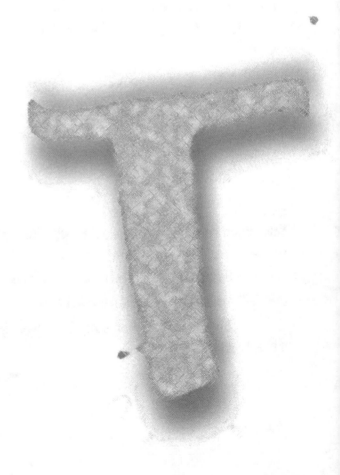

notes

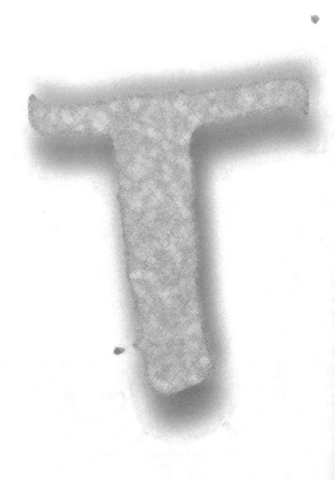

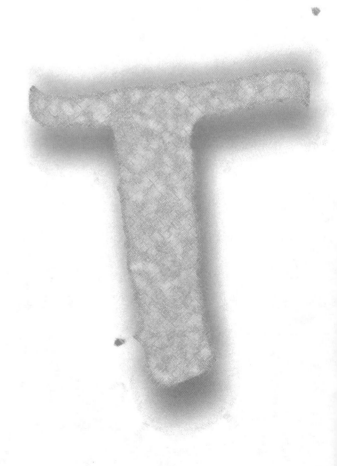

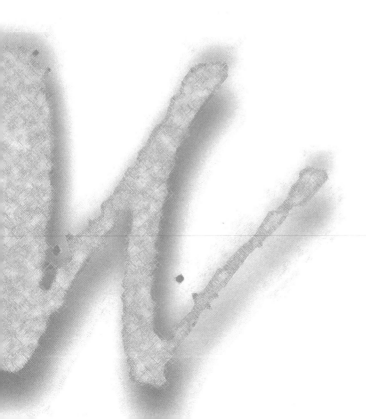

Resources from Youth Specialties

Youth Ministry Programming

Camps, Retreats, Missions, & Service Ideas (Ideas Library)

Compassionate Kids: Practical Ways to Involve Your Students in Mission and Service

Creative Bible Lessons from the Old Testament

Creative Bible Lessons in 1 & 2 Corinthians

Creative Bible Lessons in John: Encounters with Jesus

Creative Bible Lessons in Romans: Faith on Fire!

Creative Bible Lessons on the Life of Christ

Creative Bible Lessons in Psalms

Creative Junior High Programs from A to Z, Vol. 1 (A-M)

Creative Junior High Programs from A to Z, Vol. 2 (N-Z)

Creative Meetings, Bible Lessons, & Worship Ideas (Ideas Library)

Crowd Breakers & Mixers (Ideas Library) Downloading the Bible Leader's Guide

Drama, Skits, & Sketches (Ideas Library)

Drama, Skits, & Sketches 2 (Ideas Library)

Dramatic Pauses

Everyday Object Lessons

Games (Ideas Library)

Games 2 (Ideas Library)

Great Fundraising Ideas for Youth Groups

More Great Fundraising Ideas for Youth Groups

Great Retreats for Youth Groups

Holiday Ideas (Ideas Library)

Hot Illustrations for Youth Talks

More Hot Illustrations for Youth Talks

Still More Hot Illustrations for Youth Talks

Ideas Library on CD-ROM

Incredible Questionnaires for Youth Ministry

Junior High Game Nights

More Junior High Game Nights

Kickstarters: 101 Ingenious Intros to Just about Any Bible Lesson

Live the Life! Student Evangelism Training Kit

Memory Makers

The Next Level Leader's Guide

Play It! Over 150 Great Games for Youth Groups

Roaring Lambs

Special Events (Ideas Library)

Spontaneous Melodramas

Student Leadership Training Manual

Student Underground: An Event Curriculum on the Persecuted Church

Super Sketches for Youth Ministry

Talking the Walk

Teaching the Bible Creatively

Videos That Teach

What Would Jesus Do? Youth Leader's Kit

Wild Truth Bible Lessons

Wild Truth Bible Lessons 2

Wild Truth Bible Lessons—Pictures of God

Worship Services for Youth Groups

Professional Resources

Administration, Publicity, & Fundraising (Ideas Library)

Equipped to Serve: Volunteer Youth Worker Training Course

Help! I'm a Junior High Youth Worker!

Help! I'm a Small-Group Leader!

Help! I'm a Sunday School Teacher!

Help! I'm a Volunteer Youth Worker!

How to Expand Your Youth Ministry

How to Speak to Youth...and Keep Them Awake at the Same Time

Junior High Ministry (Updated & Expanded)

The Ministry of Nurture: A Youth Worker's Guide to Discipling Teenagers

Purpose-Driven Youth Ministry

Purpose-Driven Youth Ministry Training Kit

So That's Why I Keep Doing This! 52 Devotional Stories for Youth Workers

A Youth Ministry Crash Course

The Youth Worker's Handbook to Family Ministry

Discussion Starters

Discussion & Lesson Starters (Ideas Library)

Discussion & Lesson Starters 2 (Ideas Library)

EdgeTV

Get 'Em Talking

Keep 'Em Talking!

High School TalkSheets

More High School TalkSheets

High School TalkSheets: Psalms and Proverbs

Junior High TalkSheets

More Junior High TalkSheets

Junior High TalkSheets: Psalms and Proverbs

Real Kids: Short Cuts

Real Kids: The Real Deal—on Friendship, Loneliness, Racism, & Suicide

Real Kids: The Real Deal—on Sexual Choices, Family Matters, & Loss

Real Kids: The Real Deal—on Stressing Out, Addictive Behavior, Great Comebacks, & Violence

Real Kids: Word on the Street

Unfinished Sentences: 450 Tantalizing Statement-Starters to Get Teenagers Talking & Thinking

What If...? 450 Thought-Provoking Questions to Get Teenagers Talking, Laughing, and Thinking

Would You Rather...? 465 Provocative Questions to Get Teenagers Talking

Have You Ever...? 450 Intriguing Questions Guaranteed to Get Teenagers Talking

Art Source Clip Art

Stark Raving Clip Art (print)

Youth Group Activities (print)

Symbols, Phrases, and Oddities (print)

Clip Art Library Version 2.0 (CD-ROM)

Digital Resources

Clip Art Library Version 2.0 (CD-ROM)

Ideas Library on CD-ROM

Videos & Video Curricula

EdgeTV

Equipped to Serve: Volunteer Youth Worker Training Course

The Heart of Youth Ministry: A Morning with Mike Yaconelli

Live the Life! Student Evangelism Training Kit

Purpose-Driven Youth Ministry Training Kit

Real Kids: Short Cuts

Real Kids: The Real Deal—on Friendship, Loneliness, Racism, & Suicide

Real Kids: The Real Deal—on Sexual Choices, Family Matters, & Loss

Real Kids: The Real Deal—on Stressing Out, Addictive Behavior, Great Comebacks, & Violence

Real Kids: Word on the Street

Student Underground: An Event Curriculum on the Persecuted Church

Understanding Your Teenager Video Curriculum

Student Resources

Downloading the Bible: A Rough Guide to the New Testament

Downloading the Bible: A Rough Guide to the Old Testament

Grow For It Journal

Grow For It Journal through the Scriptures

Spiritual Challenge Journal: The Next Level

Teen Devotional Bible

What Would Jesus Do? Spiritual Challenge Journal

Wild Truth Journal for Junior Highers

Wild Truth Journal—Pictures of God